Online Security for the
Business Traveler

Online Security for the Business Traveler

Deborah Gonzalez
Law2sm, LLC

AMSTERDAM • BOSTON • HEIDELBERG • LONDON
NEW YORK • OXFORD • PARIS • SAN DIEGO
SAN FRANCISCO • SINGAPORE • SYDNEY • TOKYO

Butterworth-Heinemann is an imprint of Elsevier

Butterworth-Heinemann is an imprint of Elsevier
The Boulevard, Langford Lane, Kidlington, Oxford, OX5 1GB, UK
225 Wyman Street, Waltham, MA 02451, USA

Notices
Knowledge and best practice in this field are constantly changing. As new research and
experience broaden our understanding, changes in research methods, professional practices,
or medical treatment may become necessary.

Practitioners and researchers must always rely on their own experience and knowledge in
evaluating and using any information, methods, compounds, or experiments described herein.
In using such information or methods they should be mindful of their own safety and the safety
of others, including parties for whom they have a professional responsibility.

Library of Congress Cataloging-in-Publication Data
A catalog record for this book is available from the Library of Congress

British Library Cataloguing-in-Publication Data
A catalogue record for this book is available from the British Library

ISBN: 978-0-12-800069-4

For information on all Butterworth-Heinemann publications
visit our website at **http://store.elsevier.com**

This book has been manufactured using Print On Demand technology. Each copy is
produced to order and is limited to black ink. The online version of this book will show
color figures where appropriate.

CONTENTS

ABOUT THE AUTHOR

Deborah Gonzalez, Esq. is the founder of Law2sm, LLC, a legal consulting firm focusing on helping its clients navigate the legal issues relating to the new digital and social media world.

Deborah graduated from New York Law School and is licensed to practice law in New York and Georgia.

Deborah began her career in the corporate arena working in various positions in the information technology area—from network administrator to manager of the IS department for a top-6 CPA firm in New York City. During her tenure she managed day-to-day IT operations; designed and implemented IT-related training for employees, managers, and IT staff; developed policies and protocols for IT-corporate use; and monitored emerging trends for IT business strategies and management. Deborah used this foundation as a starting point with her legal practice, which is now transporting her beyond the Internet to the social space where the physical and digital dimensions of her clients coexist and where she can leverage her legal expertise to their benefit.

Deborah is a sought after speaker, content contributor, and news commentator on online security issues and social media legalities. Past audiences include Fortune 500 companies, non-profit organizations, professional associations (ISSA WIS, TAG), college communities (students, faculty, and administration), legal professionals (lawyers and judges), both domestically in the US and abroad. Specific industries include: banking and financial, healthcare and medical, higher education, international trade, governments and politicians, marketing and public relations, and more.

ONLINE RESOURCES

Thank you for selecting Butterworth-Heinemann's *Online Security for the Business Traveler*. To complement the learning experience, the author has provided a number of online tools to accompany this edition. They can be found at http://managingonlinerisk.com. The tools available include:

- Live links to chapter-specific resources and updates to case studies in the book, domestic and international.
- Downloadable handouts and checklists that you can use for your company.
- Useful infographics with additional statistics relating to online risk and security (including travel security).
- Shareable risk and security funnies and humorous videos that can be used for training or just a quick break to put things in perspective.
- *The Managing Online Risk* (MORe) monthly blog with discussions on the latest risk management and security issues (including travel security).
- An event calendar with upcoming risk and security conferences as well as the latest information regarding author tour dates and venues.
- Articles, recaps and resources regarding online travel risk and security.
- A direct contact link to the author for questions and inquiries.
- Access to the Elsevier eCommerce store for purchases.
- And more!

INTRODUCTION

Remember what Bilbo used to say: 'It's a dangerous business, Frodo, going out your door. You step onto the road, and if you don't keep your feet, there's no knowing where you might be swept off to.'

JRR Tolkien[1]

Did Tolkien know something about how travel would be in our present time (his future) that we did not? Or was he merely reflecting on one of those absolute truths that never changes throughout human history: travel can be dangerous. When transportation was by foot or horse, vulnerability was seen in terms of stamina and speed. (Can you outrun the bandit?) Boats offered ways to cross vast amounts of water space, but storms and raging waves cautioned that "there be dragons" (i.e., things you needed to look out for). (Can you swim for ten thousand leagues?) Wheels—whether by wagon, train, or cars—brought the elements of speed and weight to a dangerous level as both surpassed human capacity. (Can you withstand a push of 5–10 tons of steel against you?)

[1]Tolkien JRR. Lord of the Rings: Fellowship of the Ring; 1954.

Airplanes seem to defy gravity, but also rescue when the unfathomable happens. (Can you survive a free-fall of 30,000 ft?) But these are just the modes of transportation. Travel implies so much more.

When you go out on the road you put yourself in circumstances you did not find yourself in before—new places, new people, new cultures, new languages, new situations. Note I said, "you put yourself," for even when travel is a requirement of your position or job, you ultimately make the decision to undertake a potentially risky endeavor that could cost you your assets, your health, your sanity, your life. You come back a different person with new experiences that can alter your future—new opportunities for your company, new contacts for references, new knowledge for the future.

In representing your company outside the office you may go to conferences, internal sales meetings, external client visits, trade shows, and more. You understand that travel always includes an element of risk. But you are also high-tech enabled. When you travel you bring your smartphone, tablet, laptop, phablet, powerbook, health sensors, Google Glass, and more. These new technologies bring along new risks. Each of these devices offer productivity and efficiency through enhanced mobility and access to important documents and resources via applications and programs specifically designed to assist you in managing your company's complex and multileveled strategic goals. But these devices and apps can also become the weak link in security, leading to breaches of data and putting you and your firm in danger of material, financial, legal, and physical loss.

This book provides an overview of this mainly overlooked problem, explores some examples and cases highlighting specific security issues, and offers some practical advice on what to do differently to ensure your security while you travel and continue to engage on online activity. It offers you the most current research, insights, and best practices based on the most current and up-to-date travel-related security and risk-related articles, blogs, and surveys. That's because the book was written based on content aggregation and curation principles. In addition, you can keep your knowledge base updated using the companion website (www.managingonlinerisk.com) to get access to the latest information, data, and materials about these topics.

The structure of this book follows the travel cycle of a business executive or employee. It is intuitive in its sequence as to what steps you should take and when as you proceed on your journey. In Chapter 1, we discuss the initial decision to travel in lieu of the various alternatives for communication with colleagues across distances. With many concerns ranging from financial to security risks, executives are debating the value of travel versus online technology and digital alternatives such as Skype. However, what security risks do these alternatives present?

Chapter 2 focuses on planning, logistics, and security once the decision to travel has been made. Risks such as using online sites to purchase flights, acquiring security clothing and luggage, and downloading and using apps on your mobile devices will be explored.

Chapter 3 addresses what to do once the trip has been planned; it looks at the risks inherent in the pre-departure and departure segments of the trip. We will address security risks in terms of acquiring and preparing documentation for travel, from electronic visas and passport expediting to security measures at the airport itself, and issues in between.

Once safely arrived at the destination, security risks relating to online acquisition of currency, in-country transportation, etc., are the focus of Chapter 4. We will also discuss those pesky customs officers and the very real threat of corruption that can lead to confiscated technology and nefarious fees. Security for you, your technology, and your data is next as we discuss how to protect those through various personal health and medical management apps, Wi-Fi security awareness in foreign states and hotels, Tripit, online censorship laws, etc.

The book and our security journey ends in Chapter 5 with a review of issues and security risks involved when you return to your home or office. For example, ensuring no IT viruses or other malware traveled back with you, as well as apps that permit you to follow-up with the people you met on your travels.

Throughout the book you will be presented with various checklists, lessons learned, and resources to expand on the discussion or to provide hands-on applicability of the principles we discuss to manage online risks while conducting business travel.

So let's begin at the beginning. The first step in business travel is the decision to travel for business in the first place. With all those security and risks out there, do you really have to?

CHAPTER 1

Decision to Travel vs. Digital Alternatives

"A journey of a thousand miles begins with a cash advance."
—Anonymous[1]

Business travel can conjure up a myriad of images and feelings depending on your position (executive or employee), experience (first-timer or platinum frequent flyer), purpose (customer management or opportunity exploration), who's paying (company or self), and travel particulars (business class or economy). If that is not enough to think about, business travelers have to contend with two other concerns—safety and security (physical as well as virtual in our highly connected digital world).

Before taking a business trip, however, a critical question must be answered: Is the travel warranted. This chapter explores in depth the benefits and negatives of physical travel and contrasts them with the benefits and negatives of digital alternatives.

---

[1]Connell D. 613 Funny, inspirational and incredibly stupid travel quotes, <http://trekity.com/travel-funinspirational-travel-quotes/> [accessed 05/19/2014].

BENEFITS OF PHYSICAL TRAVEL

One would think that with the increase in cost and decrease of amenities combined with advances in visual communication technologies, physical travel would be declining. This is not the case and isn't expected to be for the foreseeable future, according to the Global Business Travel Association (GBTA) and US Travel. Table 1.1 lays out some business travel spending statistics from 2010 to 2014.[2,3,4,5,6,7,8,9] Although business trips between 2012 and 2013 dropped off slightly, business travel in 2014 is projected to surpass 2012 figures.

The question business people should ask themselves is why incur the costs of travel when there are new digital alternatives? Despite the Internet mantra, some believe they can't accomplish all of their goals online. Meeting face to face has distinct advantages when growing your business or maintaining customer satisfaction.

Table 1.1 Business Travel Spending Statistics (2010–2014)			
Year	Total Business Travel $ (in billions)	Intl Travel $ (in billions)	Total # of Business Trips (in thousands)
2010	$234		437
2011	$251	$31.6	445
2012	$262	$34.1	460
2013	$272	$34.9	453
2014	$293	$37.2	467
Note: 2014 numbers are projected estimates only.			

[2]Dooley G. Business travel outlook: moderate but steady growth, <http://www.travelagentcentral.com/trends-research/business-travel-outlook-moderate-steady-growth-34601-0>; April 11, 2012.
[3]Ibid.
[4]GBTA study finds business travel spending to grow globally, <http://www.gbta.org/foundation/pressreleases/pages/rls080513.aspx>; August 5, 2013.
[5]Business travel to fly higher in 2014, <http://www.gbta.org/foundation/pressreleases/Pages/rls_011514.aspx>; January, 2014.
[6]US travel answer sheet, <https://www.ustravel.org/sites/default/files/page/2009/11/US_Travel_Answer_Sheet_March_2013.pdf>; March 2013.
[7]US travel answer sheet, <http://www.ustravel.org/sites/default/files/page/2009/09/US_Travel_Answer Sheet_March_2014.pdf>; March 2014
[8]Business travel to fly higher in 2014, <http://www.gbta.org/foundation/pressreleases/Pages/rls_011514.aspx>; January, 2014.
[9]Beauchamp S. GBTA increases 2014 U.S. business travel spending projection, <http://www.businesstravelnews.com/More-News/GBTA-Increases-2014-U-S–Business-Travel-Spending-Projection/?a=proc>; April 8, 2014.

1. Different points in customer relations call for certain personal interactions. For example, scheduling an initial client meeting on-site signals their importance and value to your company. Also, shared experiences such as laughing together as one of you tries a new cultural food delicacy that is an acquired taste—even for the locals—builds strong relationship foundations.

2. Social gatherings outside of formal business settings are essential building blocks of mutual trust. They offer both parties an opportunity to learn more about who they are doing business with. I remember a story from a business management class about a CEO who took the final three candidates for an executive position to lunch. At the end of the lunch, he offered one of them the job. When asked what had made him choose that candidate, he said that two of the candidates put salt and pepper on their food without tasting it first. The successful candidate tasted his food and then proceeded to season. The CEO felt if the candidate would take that care in making a decision about the seasoning on his food (insignificant as that seems), he would take the time required to make the right decisions for the company.

3. A customer has to be willing and able before a sale is made. Making the right impression in person can go a long way in determining if the customer is willing to do business with us. In a World Travel and Tourism Counsel study, "executives reported that 29% of their newly obtained sales depended on employees being able to travel on behalf of the company. Additionally, business travelers themselves reported that 50% of prospective clients become customers after a trip has allowed an in-person meeting to take place, compared to the 31% who became clients without one."[10]

4. Traveling is profitable for companies. According to the World Travel and Tourism Council, "business travel improves corporate productivity and yields a return on investment of 10-to-1 and the US Travel Association found that for every dollar invested in travel, businesses benefits from an average of $12.50 in increased revenue and $3.80 in new profits."[11]

---

[10]Certify.com. The latest business travel statistics, <http://www.certify.com/2013-10-04-The-latest-business-travel-statistics#sthash.A9tFCOOC.dpuf>; October 4, 2013.
[11]Ibid.

5. Traveling can also boost productivity in the company. It creates employee bonding opportunities, allows for the exchange of fresh ideas from fresh perspectives, and provides the circumstances to enhance an employee's confidence level and overall satisfaction with his or her job by giving it purpose and recognition.[12]

NEGATIVES OF PHYSICAL TRAVEL

There are also a number of negatives to physical travel. We will discuss cost, time, the green argument, well-being, and safety and security.

Cost

Business travel is not all fun and profits. The biggest obstacle is cost—it can get expensive fast when the line items on an expense report are added up. These include:

- To-destination transportation (airlines, bus tickets, trains, etc.)
- In-destination transportation (car rentals, taxis, subway)
- Accommodations
- Per diem (meals)
- Entertaining
- Event fees
- Ancillary services (hold baggage, lockers)
- Office supplies
- Parking and gas
- Tolls
- Shipping costs of materials if sent ahead
- Cell phone usage.

Another consideration is the increase in and creation of new costs such as airline baggage fees. Unless you have a special frequent flyer status or purchased your airline ticket with a particular credit card, you will have to pay an extra fee for checked luggage. Many passengers seek to avoid the luggage fee by carrying baggage onto the plane. This often results in overhead storage bins filling up and passengers having to check-in baggage they intended to carry on—and pay a luggage fee they hoped to avoid.

[12]Seidman-Becker C. 2 Benefits of business travel you've probably never considered, <https:// www.linkedin.com/today/post/article/20130612181702-17086692-2-benefits-of-business-travel-you-ve-probably-never-considered>; June 12, 2013.

Costs, though, can be controlled to a certain extent. Check out the sidebar "Travel Savings Strategies." Preplanning can add up in savings to the bottom line. In addition, if you are self-employed, understating the IRS tax deduction permissions for business travel is essential. The second sidebar "Business Travel Tax Deduction Considerations" is a great reference. However, as with all tax codes and regulations, these change periodically. Check with your CPA before and after you travel about what is allowable and what receipts to retain.

Travel Savings Strategies

- Develop, implement, and enforce a firm travel policy.
- Require advance authorization for all business-related travel.
- Allocate reasonable per diem expense limits by destination (meals in Dubai v meals in Kansas City). Use the Federal Rate for Meals and Incidental Expenses as one guide: www.gsa.gov/perdiem (for domestic US locations) and http://aoprals.state.gov/content.asp?content_id=184&menu_id=81 (for foreign destinations).
- Negotiate rates with a hotel chain (or two) located in the majority of your destinations.
- Negotiate with one airline (or two) for corporate discounts and require employees to use that airline's booking service.
- Renegotiate with any third-party vendors supplying travel management services.
- Require employees to use public transportation and shuttle services instead of expensive taxis whenever possible.

Business Travel Tax Deductions Considerations

- The IRS standard for a tax-deductible business travel expense is "ordinary and necessary expenses that benefit or advance your business."[13]
- Examples: accommodations/hotels, meals, round-trip travel costs, in-destination transportation costs, baggage fees, and convention and seminar costs.
- Transportation costs include flights, bus rides, train trips, and auto travel.
- However, you cannot claim the price of an airline ticket if you used frequent flyer miles to acquire it.

[13]IRS. Deducting business expenses, <http://www.irs.gov/Businesses/Small-Businesses-&-Self-Employed/Deducting-Business-Expenses> [accessed 05/16/2014].

- You cannot claim expenses reimbursed to you by your company or client.
- You must be "away from home" to deduct travel expenses. Home means the area or vicinity of your principal place of business.[14]
- You can deduct up to 50% of your business-related meal costs.
- Shipping business-related materials to a meeting destination is deductible.
- Internet connection fees for business work and/or fees for business calls are deductible.
- Depending on length of travel, laundry and dry cleaning fees can be deductible.
- Conventions or business travel conducted on cruise ships have specific requirements before deductions are permitted. Review carefully.
- If your stay includes days not dedicated to work, you cannot deduct the hotel expenses or other expenses, as they would be associated with personal time. The IRS specifies that allocation of travel costs is required if personal times exceeds 25% of the total travel time.[15]
- If taking a spouse or other family member(s) along, note that those costs are not deductible unless they work for the same company and are conducting business for the company at the same time.[16]

Time

Travel can be demanding. When you are out on the road, multitasking can be extremely difficult. Consequently, part of the decision about whether to travel depends on what else you could be doing if you were not traveling. This factor requires considering schedules, priorities, and who else can do what needs to be done either at the travel location or back home.

Time management becomes essential in being able to not only complete off-site tasks but also to manage regular tasks back at the office. There are a number of time management tools and apps, but remember that these tools and apps are not enough. You also need the right resources (such as a tablet or laptop) and the right access (to the company system if you need company data for your work). These two factors bring in a number of security risks and concerns

[14]BizFilings. Business related travel expenses are deductible, <http://www.bizfilings.com/toolkit/sbg/tax-info/fed-taxes/deducting-business-related-travel-expenses.aspx>; 2012.
[15]Ibid.
[16]Bell K. Bankrate.com, Tax help for business, pleasure trips, <http://www.bankrate.com/finance/taxes/tax-help-for-business-pleasure-trips-1.aspx>; May 30, 2012.

such as lost devices, data hacking, computer scams, and more. We will discuss these in depth in Chapters 3 and 4.

The Green Argument

Some individuals believe that environmental conservation is a top value in managing their business. Reducing their company's carbon footprint, for example, may be part of the social responsibility they feel to the community. As a result, they may opt out of any business travel, especially by air, they deem excessive.

The May 2014 US National Climate Assessment report supports the relationship between air travel and carbon emissions. The report outlined specific climate change concerns and their impact on the United States. Chapter 5 states that "besides being affected by climate changes, transportation systems also contribute to changes in the climate through emissions."[17] These emissions, or carbon footprints as some call them, can accumulate quickly. For example, using a carbon footprint calculator, a recent trip from Atlanta to Los Angeles for one person with no stops equals 1514 lb of carbon dioxide.[18] "It is estimated that the average American generates about 19 tons of carbon dioxide a year; the average European, 10" in total emissions.[19] Add to this the addition statistic from the Air Transport Action Group (ATAG) that "worldwide, flights produced 689 million tons of CO_2 in 2012."[20] But these are only the totals for air travel. Additional carbon emissions are released from auto and other ground transportation as well as from ships. To calculate your own carbon footprint, see Table 1.2.

Well-Being

Another negative for business travel is its toll on individuals. Many of the aspects of traveling can lead to frustration and stress, from finding the right flight, to fighting traffic to get to the airport on time, to balancing time away from the office and time in the office, to not eating right or eating on the go, as well as time away from family, friends

---

[17]National Climate Assessment. Chapter 5 transportation, <http://nca2014.globalchange.gov>; May 2014. p. 131.

[18]<http://www.terrapass.com/carbon-footprint-calculator-2/#air> [accessed 05/16/2014].

[19]Rosenthal, E. Your biggest carbon sin may be air travel, <http://www.nytimes.com/2013/01/27/sunday-review/the-biggest-carbon-sin-air-travel.html?_r=0>; January 26, 2013.

[20]Air Transport Action Group. Facts & figures, <http://www.atag.org/facts-and-figures.html>; March 2012.

Table 1.2 Carbon Footprint Calculator Apps			
Name	**Compatible Devices**	**URL**	**Price**
My Usage Mobile	iOS & Android	https://www.myusage.com	$1.00
Zero Carbon	iPhone, iPad, iTouch	https://itunes.apple.com/us/app/zero-carbon/id336848607?mt=8	Free
SAP Carbon Track	iPhone, iPad, iTouch	https://itunes.apple.com/us/app/carbontrack/id381714512?mt=8	Free
Carbon Gobbler	iPhone, iPad	http://www.carbongobbler.com	Free
Carbon Footprint Calculator	Website	http://www.terrapass.com/carbon-footprint-calculator-2/	Free

and loved ones. The last thing you need is to end your travel by rushing to a client meeting looking like your passport picture and disheveled instead of organized, presentable, and in control.

Excessive business travel on a grueling schedule can lead to severe health conditions including anxiety, depression, extreme fatigue or chronic fatigue syndrome, migraines, weight loss, weight gain, malnutrition, vitamin deficiency, high cholesterol, diabetes, heart conditions, flu or viruses, and stomach problems. Even if you do not travel extensively or regularly, travel takes your body out of its norm. Some strategies to help offset some of these conditions include setting up an exercise routine, being conscious of nutrition while traveling, taking medications as prescribed, and learning to de-stress. I keep a little 2005 book on hand when I travel called "Travel Yoga: Stretches for Planes, Trains, Automobiles, and More!" by Darrin Zeer and Frank Montagna. It is available on Amazon for the Kindle for $5.99 or used for 1 cent + $3.99 shipping and handling.[21] I've found it useful and relaxing, even if at times I'm just laughing at the pictures knowing there is no way I'm doing that position on a plane!

Safety and Security

The last negative to discuss here is the legitimate and growing concern of physical safety while traveling abroad and the security of your company's data. Chartis, an insurance company headquartered in the United Kingdom, issued a white paper regarding pretravel risk assessments. Chartis recognized that "business travelers may encounter threats to their health, safety and security, outbreaks of civil unrest,

---

[21] Amazon. Travel yoga page, <http://www.amazon.com/Travel-Yoga-Darrin-Zeer/dp/0811845036> [accessed 05/19/2014].

terrorism, and natural disasters. With these risks in mind, it is even more important for employers to take action to protect their people. By law, an employer is bound to take reasonable care for the safety of its employees."[22] This duty of care not only requires a risk assessment before travel is undertaken so the company understands what risks may exist, but also that the employee is informed of the kind of risks he or she may face and given appropriate and sufficient information and resources to manage those risks. In addition, whereas companies previously only had to concern themselves with the safety of top executives, "companies understand now that they are liable for ALL of their traveling employees 24/7, whether they're in a business meeting or taking a side trip to run with the bulls in Pamplona."[23]

TRAVEL SECURITY PLANS

Prevention is cheaper than a travel crisis.[24]

A travel risk management and security plan provides a blueprint for everyone in the company regarding risks that may be encountered during business travel, and strategies to manage, reduce, and mitigate any damages from such risks. The plan needs to be comprehensive and cover all employees and third-party company affiliates (such as consultants) who may travel on behalf of the organization. A basic plan has the following components:

- Corporate travel policy (including preauthorization for travel).
- Training on security and safety while on business travel.
- Training on cultural aspects and business norms of the travel destination.[25]

---

[22]Chartis White Paper. Pre-travel risk assessment, <http://www.aig.com/chartis/internet/uk/eni/0109%20Lifeline%20Plus%20White%20Paper%205Aug11WEB_tcm911-360968_tcm2538-375895.pdf>; August, 2011.
[23]Carr, K. Employee safety: travel guides, <http://www.csoonline.com/article/2117733/business-continuity/employee-safety–travel-guides.html>; September 30, 2014.
[24]Ibid.
[25]A great resource that is easy to read and comprehend that I keep on my bookshelf is "Kiss, Bow and Shake Hands: Doing Business around the World," by Terri Morrison and Wayne A. Conaway, http://kissbowshakehands.com. It is a great starting point or refresher tools for some specific 60+ countries.

- Contact information of places, organizations, and people in the destination employees can contact should something occur (such as hospitals, US embassies, and hotline).
- Travel risk assessment.
- Travel risk mitigation plan.
- Global threat and warning sources (including US State Department warning subscriptions and apps approved for use by employees regarding these warnings).
- Travel insurance (including medical, kidnap, terrorism, and extra-dition, among others).
- Travel tracking systems (for reimbursements as well as employee location for safety reasons—i.e., periodic check-ins).

CORPORATE TRAVEL POLICY

A company may have more than one policy relating to business travel or may have one policy divided by sections. It is important that the policy addresses various concerns regarding travel for the employee including the rules that will govern authorization, financial matters, payments, protocols, etc. The policy should be a written document that is easily accessible to all employees in an online or electronic format. The policy should be communicated to employees through employee orientation, a formal training session or a webinar.

Most policies contain the following:

- Definition of who can travel.
- An approval process for authorizing business travel.
- Explanation of logistics to book travel.
- An overview of general risk restrictions (not specific to any particular destination).
- An outline of the noncompliance consequences employees may face for not following policy instructions.
- A list of preferred airlines, hotels, and other logistical sources/vendors—e.g., a company may have a designated travel management company (TMC) or use a corporate booking tool (CBT).
- Rules relating to electronic communication while on business travel (including hardware devices and Internet access).
- Insurance specifics for business travel.
- Travel and risk monitoring tools.

TRAVEL RISK ASSESSMENT

The best risk management strategy combines several techniques, including quality insurance coverage, sound risk management procedures and protocols, and expert advice.[26]

The travel risk assessment looks at potential risks that employees may encounter while on business travel, the likelihood of those risks occurring, the potential impact those risks may cause the business if it does occur, and the cost of implementing strategies to mitigate, reduce, or eliminate the risks.

Risk assessments can be done on two levels—one for general business travel and a second, more comprehensive one for specific travel destinations, especially if the destination is known to be hostile or dangerous.

Pretravel intelligence is very important in the second level. You need to be able to evaluate State Department warnings not just of the destination location but also of surrounding areas as spillover of dangerous activity can occur. Other types of information important to gather at this point would be "the level of political instability, the activity of terrorist organizations, the region's health hazards and the local emergency medical care, local criminal activity, and driving hazards."[27] I would add to this any censorship legislation, especially regarding Internet access and social media postings. For example, Facebook is prohibited in China.

TRAVEL SECURITY EDUCATION

Once intelligence is captured and analyzed, it needs to be conveyed to employees who will be traveling. Education on travel risk management and security is extremely important and worth the expense to the company. There are many different ways to deliver this vital information, from formal classroom training by in-house personnel to seminars led by professional travel security experts.

Exposing employees to events that did occur can shock them into awareness as to why security and safety is important. For example,

---

[26]The Ackerman Group, LLC for Chubb. Managing travel risks: tips on international business travel, <http://www.chubb.com/businesses/csi/chubb2205.pdf>; February 2014.
[27]Carr K. Employee safety: travel guides, <http://www.csoonline.com/article/2117733/business-continuity/employee-safety−travel-guides.html>; September 30, 2014.

consider the four Union Texas Petroleum employees killed by Islamic militants in Pakistan in 1997.[28] The lessons learned were not to fall into a routine and to be alert of your surroundings and who else may be around you.[29] Having the right expert present this information to your employees with the right dramatic tone can make a different impact than them just reading it.

Education can also help manage expectations of employees, some of which can be unreasonable—such as five-star quality travel accommodations and first-class air travel for a first-time customer sales call worth less than the cost of the travel. Also, employees need to be aware that they may not be able to access the Internet or information from their mobile devices[30] and should research whether there will be available low-cost global connectivity in the destination. They should also be aware of security concerns with unsecured Wi-Fi hotspots (which we discuss in Chapter 5).

DIGITAL TRAVEL ALTERNATIVES

There are many risks and many reasons about why not to travel. But if communication and interaction is important to ensure customer satisfaction and grow your business, what are the options? Here is where we are introduced to a variety of digital alternatives—some of which work better than others depending on the company's objective.

Determining if a particular digital alternative can work depends on a few variables. These include the goal for the interaction; the company's overall culture and attitude toward technology (e.g., is technology perceived as too impersonal or as a modus operandi?); the culture and attitude of technology in the organization you are interacting with; the cost of the procurement, installation, and maintenance of some of these alternatives; the strengths and reliability of the technology itself vs. its weaknesses; and security concerns regarding the platform selected.

[28]FAS. Patterns of global terrorism, Asia overview, <http://www.fas.org/irp/threat/terror_97/asia. html>; 1997.
[29]Carr K. Employee safety: travel guides, <http://www.csoonline.com/article/2117733/business-continuity/employee-safety–travel-guides.html>; September 30, 2014.
[30]Travelport. Perspectives on corporate travel trends and challenges, <http://www.travelport.com/ Travel-Trends/~/media/Corporate/Whitepapers/Perspectives%20on%20corporate%20travel%20 trends.ashx>; 2012.

The digital alternatives we will discuss go from the low tech of e-mail to the high tech of augmented reality and specific options in between, including teleconferencing, web conferencing, virtual meetings, and mixed reality.

E-mail and Asynchronous Communication

To paraphrase a common Facebook theme: click "Like" if you remember the fax machine. It is interesting to note that considering all the more advanced communications technologies that now exist, the fax is still around. It may look different—fax machines have transformed into fax apps or web sites offering fax server services, but the function is still very much a viable part of business transactions. Why? According to Fenestrea, a fax server provider, there are some very viable reasons: the fax has global coverage and acceptance, faxes are traceable, faxes are legally binding, faxes are everywhere and are established, and using faxes is easy.[31] I agree with the point that faxes are legally binding, but with all due respect to Fenestra, I believe the other points leave room for disagreement as millennials and younger generations grow up more accustomed to online digital technology platforms than push button machines. In addition, electronic signatures are being more and more accepted as proof of executed agreements for legal purposes. Concerns with these new fax servers are pretty standard in terms of any security concern with any service operating in a cloud environment: how is the data protected from unauthorized access and what controls are in place to protect privacy and confidentiality, as well as data integrity and maintenance for record keeping?[32]

Fax is also considered a one-way type of communication. It has a purpose of delivering a particular document (faster than snail mail) but not for engaging interaction. For that, we progressed to the next step—e-mail.

E-mail permits limited asynchronous communication and interaction but has its limitations. E-mail is usually not done in real time, so there is a period of time before a recipient might receive the e-mail and

---

[31]Fenestrea. 10 Reasons why fax is still important, <http://www.fenestrae.com/10-reasons-why-fax-still-important> [accessed 05/15/2014].
[32]For a good review of the top ten fax server services, see, <http://faxing-service-review.toptenreviews.com>.

then another time lapse before the recipient responds. There are occasions when the sender and the receiver may be at their devices (laptop, tablet, smartphones) at the same time when they can respond almost immediately to each other. However, not all written communication is clear, and plain text can leave a lot of the context out. Emoticons— smiley faces and the like—were created to add some of the missing context. The differences in time zones can also give an illusion of e-mail being spontaneous—such as sending an e-mail before retiring at night and waking up to find the response from across the world.

E-mails, like faxed documents, are also considered legal to a certain extent as they are used as evidence during e-discovery or the electronic discovery process in investigations and litigations. As for security, the same concerns apply as with most data systems, except that most e-mail systems are internal to the company and so the company has more control over protecting its contents and access to the accounts.

Teleconferencing

Using the phone to interact with employees, clients, vendors, and others seems more direct in terms of real-time discussion and collaborating on business tasks and projects. It permits participants to engage with each other from multiple locations convenient to them and across multiple time zones. Scheduling can be difficult because of different time zones, but it does save on time and expense that would have been used to physically travel for an in-person meeting. For some, however, teleconferencing offers half a solution: participants can hear each other but they cannot see each other, missing out on nuanced body language and other nonverbal signals that add context to the conversation. Also, because everyone is disbursed and can't see each other, interruptions and speaking over each other are common problems. Some examples of teleconferencing services include:

- Google ChromeBox ($99): http://www.theverge.com/2014/2/6/5386582/ google-takes-on-business-teleconferencing-with-999-chromebox-for
- AT&T Conferencing Services: http://www.business.att.com/enterprise/Family/unified-communications/conferencing-services/
- Skype—a freemium voice-over-IP service and instant messaging client, currently developed by the Microsoft Skype Division: http://www.skype.com/en/

As we mention Skype, here are a few things to note. Skype does offer video conferencing, so you can see as well as hear participants. It can be used across different platforms and devices (smartphones, tablets, etc.) and can offer good quality depending on your Internet service provider (ISP). However, there is a fee for more than two participants, you need a fast broadband connection, and it has been known to crash. In addition, Skype is considered a social media network—meaning it is not on a private or secure channel. Accordingly, confidential information should not be discussed on this platform.

Web Conferencing and Virtual Meetings

Web conferencing permits users to use a web-based application to conduct virtual meetings combining real-time sound and video (including movement and document sharing). For corporate use, these can be much more formal and expensive but offer additional security controls. For tips on running successful virtual meetings, see the Sidebar.

- WebEx—http://www.webex.com, Cisco Systems. This virtual meeting application can be used on various platforms and devices, offers password protection for meeting and materials access, and allows sharing of desktops, etc. This service can be expensive if used extensively and, since the meeting is hosted on their site, is vulnerable to crashes, etc.
- GoTo Meeting—http://www.gotomeeting.com, Citrix. This is a high-definition web conferencing and online meeting tool. It also has a version to provide virtual webinars and online training.
- Google Plus Hangout—https://plus.google.com/hangouts, Google. This is an informal social media platform that permits multiple participants to conduct fun, group, live conversations. Keep in mind that this is an open platform, so security concerns make it an unlikely "official" choice for business users. But that won't stop employees who like using Google Hangouts from hanging out with friends who may be colleagues, customers, or vendors. Consequently, it should be addressed in the security and risk management plans.

●●●――――――――――――――――――――――――――――――――

Tips on Running Successful Virtual Meetings

- Have all participants test the system on the device they will use for the virtual meeting before the meeting is to take place.

- Send out an agenda (and any required reading materials) before the meeting so participants are prepared with whatever information or reports they are supposed to share.
- Limit the participants and the meeting duration.
- Make sure everyone introduces himself or herself at the start of the meeting. If someone joins late, make an announcement that the person has joined but do not start introductions again.
- Set meeting ground rules up front. Include technology instructions such as mute buttons, raising the hand icons, and silencing cell phones.
- Poll the virtual meeting periodically to make sure everyone is paying attention and engaged.
- Use names during the meeting so people can keep track of who is saying what.[33]

Mixed Reality

Mixed reality is when elements from the real world are combined with elements of a virtual world to allow real-time interaction in an environment that does not exist. Some of you might think of the Holographic Environment Simulator (Holodeck) in the Star Trek series that permitted Star Fleet personnel to engage in different activities based on simulated environments. As a digital alternative to business travel, mixed reality has progressed from simple avatar-type methodologies to full-range conference and event services.

Let me introduce you to the Virtualis Center.[34] Virtualis founder Dan Parks was intrigued with the virtual 3D world Second Life, which was created by Linden Labs in 1999 and opened to the public in 2003 as a gaming platform.[35] In April 2008, Parks opened a Conference Center in Second Life to offer "businesses new, stimulating, low-cost venues for meetings."[36] The center has evolved to offer more than 29,000 m^2 of virtual meeting space in its conference center and grand ballroom with zero carbon emissions. Clients can request various services from Virtualis' seasoned team of event planning professionals. These include:

---

[33]Adapted from various online sources, including: The Info Tech Research Group. Best Practice Checklist for virtual Meetings, <http://www.infotech.com/research/best-practice-checklist-for-virtual-meetings>; February 14, 2006.
[34]Home page. <http://corporateplanners.com/VIRTUALIS.asp>.
[35]Home page. <http://secondlife.com>.
[36]Stewart C. Second life convention center shows virtual meeting pros and cons, <http://www.ocregister.com/articles/second-16542-life-virtual.html>; April 24, 2008.

- Custom-designed meetings, team-building, and networking events.
- Powerful agendas with specific attention to detail and logistics based upon in-world knowledge.
- Organizational branding.
- Sponsorship development.
- Procurement of real-life speakers and entertainment.
- Custom or generic avatars.
- Training to maximize a positive in-world experience.
- Risk and security assessment to protect proprietary information.
- On-site technical and logistical support throughout the entire virtual event.
- Post-Event Evaluations to assess Return on Investment (ROI) for compliance with Sarbanes-Oxley.[37]

Your company may not be ready for this kind of artificial reality, but we may see more of these kinds of virtual venues develop and become popular with the millennials and younger generations who have been raised on virtual gaming platforms.

Before we leave this section on physical travel vs. digital alternatives, note Table 1.3, which provides some information about current travel risk and security apps that you, your company, and your employees may find helpful. As with all app listings, apps may be discontinued or their price may be increased.

Table 1.3 Travel Risk and Security Apps			
Name	Compatible Devices	URL	Price
US Dept. Smart Traveler	iOS & Android	http://www.corporatetravelsafety.com/safety-tips/category/cell-phone-travel-apps/tip/test	Free
Overseas Security	iPhone, iPad	http://www.overseassecurity.com	Free
React Mobile	iOS & Android	http://reactmobile.com	Free
Emergensee Personal Safety System	iOS & Android	http://emergensee.com/emergensee-featured-onetravel-com/	Free
AON WorldAware	iOS & Android	http://www.aon.com/risk-services/crisis-management/worldaware/downloads.jsp	$7.99

[37]Home page. <http://corporateplanners.com/VIRTUALIS.asp>.

CHAPTER 2

Planning, Logistics, and Security

No matter how you travel, it's still you going.
—Jeff Goldblum[1]

The decision to travel has been made, and the authorization given. Now planning begins in earnest. Depending on your schedule and resources, this may be the least enjoyable part of the experience. Planning business travel can be tedious, time consuming, and frustrating. Online web sites and mobile apps often promise an easy, convenient, cost-conscious way to set your agenda. But buyer beware! Digital tools can lead to security and safety risks—from lost devices to socially engineered hacking attacks that target you and your data. A rule of thumb is to consider potential security risks you may face at each step in planning and finalizing your itinerary. Here's something else to remember: If you are not the one planning the trip, review plans presented to you with security in mind. Better yet, discuss security with the person planning your trip before they begin making travel arrangements. This chapter discusses some of the risks of online travel purchasing, the protection certain apparel and luggage offer, and

---

[1]Travel Quotes, <http://www.vagabondroots.com/travel-quotes/> [accessed 06/08/2014].

reliable online resources and apps that provide valuable information to assess and mitigate potential problems

PURCHASING ONLINE AND SECURITY

How many TV, radio, and Internet commercials bombard us daily touting online travel web sites, as a great way to obtain high-quality transportation and lodging at a fabulous price? Some of the more common and popular sites are (more can be seen in Table 2.1):

- Expedia   http://www.expedia.com
- Kayak   http://www.kayak.com
- Orbitz   http://www.orbitz.com
- Priceline   http://www.priceline.com
- Travelocity   http://www.travelocity.com

Each makes the same claim: the lowest price available for your desired destination and at your desired comfort or luxury level. Just put in your travel information and ... voila! Suddenly you have lists to scroll through and select from. You even have the option of registering on the site, of saving the itinerary that you select, and returning to the site for additional statistics on your travel data, all neatly accumulated and formatted. But the data is also saved. At this

Table 2.1 Travel Saving Apps and Web Sites			
Name	Compatible Devices	URL	Price
WhichAirline	iOS & Android	http://www.whichairline.com	Free
Google Flight Explorer	iOS & Android	www.google.com/flights	$3.99
ThePointsGuy.com	Web site	http://thepointsguy.com	Free
Altimeter	Web site	http://appadvice.com/appguides/show/altimeter-elevation-apps	Free
What's App	iOS & Android	http://www.whatsapp.com	Free
Google's Field Trip	iOS & Android	https://play.google.com/store/apps/details?id=com.nianticproject.scout&hl=en	Free
Hitlist	iOS & Android/ Facebook	http://www.hitlistapp.com	Free
Momondo	iOS & Android/ Facebook	http://www.momondo.com	Free

point, a security-minded person should ask, saved where? This is an important question because you have no control of the security of the location where your data is saved (on the cloud, in a remote server). Access to that data (whether authorized or not) is also out of your control. You have to trust that these web sites have put into place appropriate security controls to protect your information—from financial information used to purchase travel services to personally identifiable information such as user IDs and passwords.

A few questions to ask before using one of these web sites:

1. Has your company authorized employees to use these sites for business travel? Or, does your company use a specific travel management company?
2. Does the web site adhere to PCI Data Security Standards (DSS) from the Security Standards Council? https://www.pcisecuritystandards.org/security_standards/
3. Does the web site have a secured portal for transactions, usually identified with a "https"?
4. Does the web site have security policies (sometimes found on their Terms of Use page)?
5. Does the web site have security disclaimers?
6. Has the web site been breached before?

Even though the travel web sites I listed relate to air travel, keep in mind that the same security concerns exist for any transportation web site—Amtrak (railroad), Greyhound (buses), Carnival Cruise lines (ships), etc. If you plan, book, and save purchases for travel or related items such as rentals for cars, bikes, canoes, etc., online, it is important to give careful consideration to security controls that may or may not exist.

Business travelers should also have the same security concerns about privacy and protection of personal and financial data when making lodging arrangements. There are a variety of web sites that provide information about hotel rooms, hotel direct web sites, or web sites that offer the option of being able to share a couch or room in a private home. These include:

- Airbnb   https://www.airbnb.com
- Hotels.com   http://www.hotels.com
- Trivago   http://www.trivago.com

Security professionals emphasize the importance of strong passwords for travel accounts as a first step to protect yourself and your data. Strong passwords reduce the risk of a security breach because they include an unpredictable mix of symbols, numbers, and upper and lowercase letters. You can increase password strength by not sharing the password among your other accounts. In addition, using biometrics or two-factor verification that require additional information in order to access your account is also highly recommended. Another strategy is to create a temporary e-mail address and password to be used only for a particular instance of business travel and then terminate the e-mail and password once the travel is completed. You could also create an e-mail and password only for travel.

ORGANIZING THE PLAN AND LOGISTICS

It's been said that the only thing tougher than managing employee travel is handing out assigned parking spaces in the company lot.[2]

Purchasing services is just one step in business travel. Travel logistics communications such as tickets and lodging confirmations are usually electronic and tend to be distributed to the parties who need to know by electronic means such as e-mail or mobile apps. Organizing all the information about a trip in one location is a time management strategy that has security implications. An example is the iPhone's Passport app. Just one of a wide collection of travel-related apps, Passport "keeps things like airline boarding passes, movie tickets, and gift cards all in one place, letting you scan your iPhone or iPod touch to check-in for a flight, get into a movie, redeem a coupon, and more.[3]" Table 2.2 lists some others.

Having all of the information about a business trip in one place is convenient but also provides a hacker with a one-stop shop. When you couple this reality with the ubiquitous use of mobile devices, it's easy to understand why corporate risk management is placing growing importance on mobile security.

[2]Entrepreneur.com. The myths and realities of Internet travel, <http://www.entrepreneur.com/article/205222#>; July 1, 2010.
[3]Apple Passport Information Web site, <http://support.apple.com/kb/HT5483?viewlocale=en_US&locale=en_US> [accessed 06/08/2014].

Table 2.2 Travel Itinerary and Organization Apps			
Name	**Compatible Devices**	**URL**	**Price**
TripIt	iOS & Android	https://www.tripit.com	Free
TripCase	iOS & Android	http://travel.tripcase.com	Free
WorldMate	iOS & Android	https://www.worldmate.com	$3.99
GateGuru	iOS & Android	http://www.gateguru.com	Free
Awesome Note	iPhone	http://www.bridworks.com/anote/eng/	$3.99

Critical security questions to consider regarding apps and mobile devices before taking a business trip include:

1. Does your company have a policy for mobile security?
2. Does your company have lists of approved and/or prohibited apps?
3. Does your company have mobile security controls—such as security software, apps, or protocols that can be put on your device(s)?
4. Are the apps you plan to use free or do they have a fee? Apps that are free usually make their money by "sharing" your information. Apps that have a fee tend not to share information since they have a revenue stream.[4]

WARNINGS

Travel is fatal to prejudice, bigotry, and narrow-mindedness.
—Mark Twain[5]

Once the destination is known, information regarding risks associated with the location should be identified and reviewed. Table 2.3 lays out some of the resources available online and at no or low cost that should be consulted.

Preparation for a trip includes not only reviewing information regarding your destination but also reviewing general travel security and safety materials. Some are available online or in a classroom setting. Some companies such as E-TravelSafety provide travel

---

[4]Rosenbloom S. How not to pay the price for free Wi-Fi, <http://www.nytimes.com/2014/06/08/travel/how-not-to-pay-the-price-for-free-wi-fi.html?ref=technology&_r=0&gwh=E9D21CCFAA53A3BB08663051F108D39A&gwt=pay&assetType=nyt_now>; June 8, 2014.

[5]613 Funny, Inspirational and Incredibly Stupid Travel Quotes, Compiled by Darcie Conned, <http://trekity.com/travel-funinspirational-travel-quotes/> [accessed 05/19/2014].

Table 2.3 Travel Warning, Health and Safety Resources			
Name	**Url**	**Comments**	**Misc.**
Corporate Travel Safety	www.corporatetravelsafety.com	Safety Tips for Business Travelers	
Nations Online Project	http://www.nationsonline.org/oneworld/travel_warning.htm	Collects travel warnings from around the world.	
US Dept. of State: Bureau of Consular Affairs	http://travel.state.gov/content/travel/english.html	Mission: Safety. Security. Service. Our highest priority is to protect the lives and interests of US citizens overseas. We do this through routine and emergency services to Americans at our embassies and consulates around the world. We serve our fellow citizens during their most important moments—births, deaths, disasters, arrests, and medical emergencies.	Beyond just passports. Includes information about finding medical assistance abroad and locations of US consulates and embassies.
Travel Health Online	https://www.tripprep.com/scripts/main/default.asp	Guide to health and safety in more than 220 countries, including vaccine and immunization information as well as medical assistance contacts.	Provided by Shoreland, Inc.
US Center for Disease Control (CDC)	http://wwwnc.cdc.gov/travel/destinations/list	Provides traveler's health information by country.	
World Health Organization (WHO)	http://www.who.int/countries/en/	Provides health information by country.	

security and safety training. E-TravelSafety offers e-learning courses focusing on travel security and safety that businesses can customize depending on the travel destination. Stuart Anderson, their director, talks about how technology enhances travel safety and security in the sidebar.

●●●
──

E-TravelSafety Interview

Stuart Anderson, MSc

Director, www.e-travelsafty.com

Tell Me a Bit About Yourself and Your Company

Over the past two decades, I have obtained a wealth of experience in travel security, from providing diplomatic protection to operating in remote and hostile environments. During this time, I have developed and delivered different travel security packages to a diverse mix of clients from overseas embassies to an oil major.

The business travel experience and the way business is conducted internationally have changed since the events of the World Trade Center. Countries that were once considered only for those with a high-risk appetite are now opening up to a wider sphere of trade. Through developments in technology and communication tools such as Skype, companies can easily conduct business around the world. This does not mean that business travel has been reduced, but it does mean that the approach to travel has changed.

Understanding the trends associated with travel security has allowed e-travelsafety.com to develop and provide the business community with a cost-effective and hassle-free travel safety product. We have designed a cloud-based travel safety solution that could be used for any business traveler. It provides everything a traveler could need—from a pretravel risk assessment to guidelines to how to react in an emergency. This allows a corporate organization to deliver its duty of care for its employees by providing relevant travel security training on a scalable basis.

How Has Online Technology Changed the World of Business Travel?

In the last decade, a wealth of travel information services has become available to assist the business traveler. These services mostly stem from open source information on the Internet and from credible sources such as the FCO and CIA fact book web sites. They have further developed in the last 3–5 years with the use of mobile applications that can track, communicate, and provide information and advice to the business traveler. The result is a good set of tools to assist the business traveler, but they can sometimes offer a false hope by creating an overreliance on technology without an understanding of the basic fundamentals of safety and security.

I believe these tools should be used in addition to effective pretravel training. A foundational understanding of travel security is essential if a business traveler loses a phone or is unable to access these tools.

What Trends Do You See in Online Technology for Business Travel?

The further development of mobile applications and extended travel tracking services will be a natural progression for most business travelers. I also see online pretravel training and advice developing to align more closely with the corporate traveler's experience.

Is Safety the Same as Security When it Comes to Online and Business Travel?

Although safety and security are two different topics, they are very closely related when it comes to business travel. A weakness in security increases risk, which in turn decreases safety. Travel safety, however, covers nonsecurity-related risks that can include health and basic safety concerns.

Has Online Technology Added New Security Concerns to Business Travel?

Online technology has developed to the point that the business traveler can rely solely on that and fail to understand the fundamentals of travel security. However, social media has created new concerns about the lack of privacy around personal and business travel. Tweeting your way through Mexico City or posting your pictures on Instagram when you are by the pool in the Middle East can cause offence or raise your profile for a kidnap for ransom attempt. When I first started teaching Travel Security, these social media sites were not available, and it was easy to keep a low profile while traveling. Now it is harder simply because of the way we communicate.

How Does Your Product Address These Security Concerns?

Our e-learning travel safety package includes a pretravel course that provides practical and interactive advice that addresses all of these concerns. The course covers all the points a traveler will need to stay safe. It is available year-round, even during a trip.

What Sources Would You Recommend (Books, Web sites, Linkedin Groups, Companies, Individuals) to Study Online Security for Business Travelers?

Do your research prior to traveling and test apps before leaving home to familiarize yourself with their strengths and weaknesses. I would also recommend using online travel guides and interactive packages. A book is a good source, but travel safety is not seen as the most interesting subject. I think interactive online learning provides the best user experience.

Do You Have a Quote Regarding Online (Business) Travel and Security/Risk?

Always undertake pretravel planning.

LUGGAGE AND SECURITY

Did you ever notice that the first piece of luggage on the carousel never belongs to anyone?

—Erma Bombeck[6]

Most people would say they make decisions about what they wear and the luggage in which they carry what they wear based on function or fashion. For business travelers, function involves more than carrying your stuff. It also means securing your stuff, especially devices and data. A number of companies specialize in travel gear with antitheft technology. For example, Pacsafe (www.pacsafe.com) offers "smart travel gear" from wallets to handbags, backpacks to luggage, laptop cases to camera cases, and anything in between you can think of. They also have a variety of Radio Frequency Identification (RFID)-blocking wallets and organizers (http://www.pacsafe.com/travel-accessories-wallets/rfid-blocking.html) you can wear in a variety of places on your body. Travelsmith (www.travelsmith.com) does not manufacture safe gear but is a retailer of various safe gear products by different manufacturers and a good resource for price and option comparisons.

One of the key pieces of luggage for many business travelers is the carry-on, which not only holds your things but saves you time during ticket check-in and departure since you are not checking-in and retrieving your bag. Reliable and sturdy carry-ons or wheelers can cost more than $200. Carry-on bags are available with an array of secure features. The more secure the bag, the more it will cost.

Another luggage security feature focuses on locks. Some locks have a "TSA-friendly" label. These can include combination locks, locks with wire cables, and/or luggage straps. I can envision a future generation of digital electronic and wireless locks that connect to a mobile device on the luggage.

Here are some key factors to consider when purchasing luggage:

- Size (to fit airline specifications)—include wheels and handles as part of the size.
- Expansion and compression.
- Rollers (two wheels) vs. Spinners (roll upright; four wheels).

---

[6]Goodreads Quotes on Travel, <http://www.goodreads.com/quotes/tag/travel?page=2> [accessed 06/08/2014].

- Hard-sided vs. soft.
- Exterior and interior pockets and brackets.
- Warranties (limited vs. lifetime).
- Locks: type and if provided.
- Luggage ID options.
- Travel habits (frequency, transportation preferences).[7]

WEARABLES AND SECURITY

It is interesting to note that the current trend in wearable technologies allows self-monitoring for health as well as for competitive purposes. These technologies will only improve in the future, become more pervasive (read: invisible to the naked eye), and create a number of security and privacy concerns. Google Glass brought some of these issues to light since its controversial debut and continues to do so.[8] Others also see potential in wearable technology for identification and verification of identity to enhance security. For example, Bionym's Nymi bracelet uses the electrocardiogram (ECG) of its wearer for authentication.[9] A low-cost alternative is the NFC Ring, successfully funded via a Kickstarter campaign in 2013. The ring allows you to interact with other NFC-connected devices.[10]

Popular wearables in the health and fitness market—from bracelets to sensors that connect wirelessly or via Wi-Fi to mobile devices—focus on giving feedback to the wearer regarding their health and fitness levels. According to this concept of the "monitored man," these wearables assist the user in achieving health and fitness goals. There have been privacy concerns regarding where this information is stored and who the apps may share the information with. Is the information, for example, shared with health insurance companies?

A growing security concern of these wearables is whether they would disclose an executive's specific location should the device be

---

[7]Stellin S. How to choose a carry-on bag, <http://www.nytimes.com/2013/12/01/travel/how-to-choose-a-carry-on-bag.html?nl=todaysheadlines&emc=edit_th_20131130> November 27, 2013.
[8]Vacar T. Google Glass certain to impact privacy laws, <http://www.ktvu.com/news/news/local/google-glass-certain-impact-privacy-laws/nfbyj/>; April 16, 2014.
[9]Nymi Home Page, <http://www.bionym.com/tech/> [accessed 06/08/2014].
[10]NFC Ring Kickstarter Page, <https://www.kickstarter.com/projects/mclear/nfc-ring> [accessed 06/08/2014].

hacked. If an unauthorized person gained access to the device, the wearer could be vulnerable to being attacked or kidnapped.

As a chapter recap, here is a checklist to plan your business travel. In Chapter 3, we will continue our journey with advice about predeparture preparations and departure security concerns.

●●●——————————————————————————————————

Checklist: Planning

Gather Travel Documents
- Passport or Passport Card, Visas, Special Permits.
- Tickets (or e-tickets), Lodging Reservations and Confirmations.
- ID cards: Driver's licenses, traveler's checks, credit card information.
- Photocopies: One for yourself and one for a trusted friend, family member, or coworker.

Check Destination Information
- Travel Warnings vs. Public Announcement (short term).
- US Department of State: Consular Information Sheets. (http://travel.state.gov/content/passports/english/country.html).
- Overseas Security Advisory Council (OSAC) Crime and Safety Reports. https://www.osac.gov/pages/Home.aspx
- Other Countries' Travel Information Sites.
  - United Kingdom https://www.gov.uk/foreign-travel-advice
  - Canada http://travel.gc.ca/travelling/advisories
  - Australia http://www.smartraveller.gov.au
- Identify and keep on hand Country Embassy/Consulate Location
  - US citizens can register in the Smart Traveler Enrollment Program (STEP) at https://step.state.gov/step/, a free service to allow US citizens and nationals traveling abroad to enroll their trip with the nearest US Embassy or Consulate. Provided by the US Department of State, Bureau of Consulate Affairs.
- Cultural and Business Norms
  - The Destination Country's Government Web site.
  - Laws of the destination country (ex. bribery).
    - CIA's World Factbook https://www.cia.gov/library/publications/the-world-factbook/
- Health Concerns—Visit travel clinic or doctor
  - Update prescriptions and keep medical prescription information with other important documents.
  - Have information about where to find medical assistance in the destination.
  - Check CDC or WHO for health warnings and get vaccines if required and/or recommended.

Review Company Travel Materials and Policies

- Company's Travel Policy (including reimbursement requirements).
- Company's Travel Risk Assessment.
  - Company property vs. personal property.
- Company's Travel Safety and Emergency Protocols.
  - Travel Risk Management (TRM) Services.[11]
- Attend or participate in a company Travel Safety Training (if provided for).

Review and Acquire Insurance

- Health/Medical.
  - Medical Evacuation.
- Overseas/Travel Insurance.
- Company Insurance for Theft.

---

[11]An example is iJet International's TRAVELER 2 Mobile App: <www.ijet.com>. iJET's end-to-end, tailored solution integrates world-class threat intelligence, innovative technology and global response services that help enterprises protect their people and operational assets and mitigate operational risk. Another is i-Care by TMC Inntel <http://www.inntel.co.uk>. More on these in Chapter 4.

CHAPTER 3

Predeparture and Departure

Airplane travel is nature's way of making you look like your passport photo.
—Al Gore[1]

The tickets have been purchased and travel apps with the relevant details loaded onto your mobile devices. Now come some of the most tedious aspects of your trip—assembling the necessary government documentation, packing, and getting through airport security. As you go through the predeparture ritual, arrive at the transportation hub, and actually depart, digital security concerns and risks follow you in your mobile devices and electronic interactions. This chapter looks at those risks and ways to mitigate them as you run from the taxi to the terminal to the departure gate and then board and settle into your seat on the aircraft.

[1]613 Funny, Inspirational and Incredibly Stupid Travel Quotes, Compiled by Darcie Conned, <http://trekity.com/travel-funinspirational-travel-quotes/> [accessed 05/19/2014].

PASSPORTS, VISAS, ONLINE, OH MY

Air travel—whether for business or pleasure—requires specific official documentation. Identification is one of them. Domestically, most airlines permit US citizens to travel with a valid photo identification card—driver's license, nondriver's license, etc. Sometimes for air travel to US territories, such as Puerto Rico, all that is required is a valid photo-ID and a copy of your birth certificate. For international travel, however, a government-issued passport (or in the United States, a passcard) is the standard. Information about acquiring a US passport is available at the US Department of State, Bureau of Consulate Affairs web site: http://travel.state.gov/content/passports/english.html. Although the web site provides essential information and is a great place to start the process, you must apply for a passport in person at a Department of State Passport Agency or an Authorized Passport Acceptance Facility. If you are located outside the United States and are a US citizen, you need to go to the US Embassy or Consulate located in the country where you are living or visiting.[2] This is important to know in case you lose your passport while overseas or your passport expires while you are traveling abroad. The web site also allows you to monitor your passport application status.

As with other online web sites, breached or hacked personal data pose constant security risks. The US Department of State, as with other Federal Agencies, is covered under The Comprehensive National Cybersecurity Initiative (CNCI). The CNCI, which was implemented under former President George W. Bush's administration in 2008 and expanded by President Obama's administration in 2013,[3] has 12 specific initiatives, including:

- Manage the Federal Enterprise Network as a single network enterprise with Trusted Internet Connections.
- Deploy an intrusion detection system of sensors across the Federal enterprise.

[2]US Dept. of State, BCA Website, <http://travel.state.gov/content/passports/english/passports/applying-for-a-u-s-passport-from-outside-the-united-states.html> [accessed 06/09/2014].
[3]Comprehensive National Cybersecurity Initiative web site, <http://www.whitehouse.gov/issues/foreign-policy/cybersecurity/national-initiative> [accessed 06/09/2014].

- Coordinate and redirect research and development (R&D) efforts.
- Define and develop enduring "leap-ahead" technology, strategies, and programs.

In addition to a passport, entry to a particular country may require a travel visa granted by that country's government. Like a passport, there are a variety of ways to obtain the visa. More and more countries are providing online portals for obtaining the visa or at least to begin the process. The Republic of Turkey has an electronic visa application system (e-visa) where you can apply, pay the fee, and download the e-visa (https://www.evisa.gov.tr/en/). The e-visas are not available to everyone as there are certain country restrictions, and you need to qualify with specific verifiable documents.

For US citizens wishing to travel to India, Tranvisa is the outsourced visa application service agency (https://indiavisa.travisaoutsourcing.com/). However, unlike the Turkey process, you can begin the visa process online but need to snail mail your US passport to a specific Indian consulate in the United States to obtain it. Applying for a visa to the Russian Federation is also hybrid—part online and part snail mail of required documentation (https://visa.kdmid.ru/).

Then there are specific international visa service organizations that offer to do the work for you, for a fee of course. Some of these include Visalady.com, International Visa Service, Perry International Visa Service, and PVS International. Others can be found by googling the country name with "visa" in the search query.

One last document to be aware of is the International Drivers Permit (IDP).[4] Some people want to drive when they reach their location, but many countries do not recognize another country's drivers license. However, more than 180 countries accept an IDP. In the United States, applications are processed through the American Automobile Association (AAA). You can download the application online and mail it with the fee (currently $15).[5] Processing takes 4−6 weeks, and the IDP is valid for 1 year.

---

[4]US Government Answers web site, <http://answers.usa.gov/system/templates/selfservice/USAGov/#!portal/1012/article/2815/International-Driving-Permit-IDP> [accessed 06/09/2014].
[5]AAA IDP Application Form, <http://www.aaa.com/vacation/idpapplc.html?association=undefined&clb_id=undefined&secure=N> [accessed 06/09/2014].

Keep in mind that anytime you submit information online you may expose yourself to a security risk. The information is captured and stored somewhere, which increasingly is the cloud. Not all government and private agencies processing passports, visas, and driver permits have the same level of security controls as mandated by the US government. So, you have to decide between the convenience of applying online and the security of applying in person. One other note, some government agencies no longer accept in-person applications. Check with the country's consulate for specific application instructions.

PACKING AND SECURITY

When preparing to travel, lay out all your clothes and all your money. Then take half the clothes and twice the money.
—*Susan Heller[6], NYT*

In Chapter 2, we looked at travel luggage. Here, we will discuss what to put in that luggage. There is no doubt one of two things will happen, it will not all fit or you will forget something. Or, you may make a mistake like I once did—I checked off everything on my packing list, got to my hotel, and took out a pair of heels only to discover that one was black and the other one blue!

On the bright side, a number of web sites provide packing lists as well as a selection of apps. Some are listed in Table 3.1. Besides the appropriate apparel (remember to consider the weather of the destination country[7]), and toiletries, do not forget your devices and security tools—such as flash drives, hardware keys, and RFID wallets. Another good thing to put in place are smartphone alerts to remind

Table 3.1 Travel Packing and Reminder Apps			
Name	Compatible Devices	URL	Price
TravelList	iPhone	http://travellistapp.com	$1.99
Packing Pro	iPhone	http://www.quinnscape.com/PackingPro.asp	$2.99
Trip List	iPhone	http://triplistapp.com/ea/	Free/$2.99 Pro

[6]Heller S. Half the clothes twice the money travel blog, <http://halftheclothesandtwicethemoney. blogspot.com> [accessed 06/09/2014].
[7]The Weather Channel has an app for that, <http://www.weather.com/services/mobilesplash. html> [accessed 06/09/2014].

you of not just times but also to remember certain documents such as your passport and/or visas.

PREPARING DEVICES FOR SECURED TRAVEL

For most of us, leaving behind our electronic devices (laptops, tablets, smartphones) is not an option. So, understanding how to protect these devices is a security best practice, especially since numerous incidences of searches and seizures of electronic gear at international borders have led to compromised data and even loss of devices. The following questions will help you determine what items to take and how to secure them:

1. What data do I really need?
   a. Traveling with a bare or "forensically clean" device.[8]
   b. Secure portable data storage devices that are small and easily hidden.
2. How can I protect that data and/or the device carrying the data?
   a. Back up the data.
   b. Encryption.
   c. Locks—Hardware; beyond simple passwords; biometrics.
   d. Turn off the devices to wipe out volatile memory.
   e. Install tamperproof seals or glitter nail polish.[9]
3. What are the alternatives to carrying this data?
   a. Secure remote access.
   b. Secure cloud-hosted content.
   c. Surveillance concerns.
4. What is the impact to my company or myself if the data is disclosed or seized?
   a. Travel and data insurance.
   b. Incident reporting for compliance regulations.
   c. Loss of customer trust.

SECURING THE OFFICE WHEN YOU TRAVEL

Although often overlooked, securing your office space while you travel is very important. Your physical absence can provide opportunities for

[8]Benetton L. How to secure your laptop before crossing the border, Canadian Bar Association, <http://www.cba.org/cba/Practicelink/tayp/laptopborder.aspx> [accessed 06/05/2014].
[9]Borland J. Don't want your laptop tampered with? Just add glitter nail polish, <http://www.wired.com/threatlevel/2013/12/better-data-security-nail-polish/>; December 30, 2013.

old-fashioned on-site theft or modern digital espionage. The following best practices can help you secure your office and data while you are away on business:

- Make sure your company IT department knows you will be traveling so they can monitor any inappropriate activity from your desktop or company accounts.
- Discuss with IT any remote access options so they can be sure it is you who is accessing the company network and you can get the access you need with little hassle.
- Secure and lock all digital equipment.
- Change the password on your desktop computer.
- Put away and lock any confidential information—such as client information or information regarding your specific travel arrangements.
- Only permit access to your office and its contents by a trusted source—such as an assistant—by giving them a key (physical or digital). Limit the keys you distribute.
- Instead of an "out of office" e-mail auto response, have your assistant access your e-mails, access them from your destination, or put in a more general "busy message" to minimize the number of people who know you are traveling.
- Many voice mail systems will convert a voice message to a text-based message and e-mail it to you. This is another way to avoid the "out of office" message.
- Have an assistant hold your mail or, if you have a home office, have the Post Office temporarily hold your mail or forward to a specific address.

TSA SECURITY

Travel, in the younger sort, is a part of education; in the elder, a part of experience.

—Francis Bacon[10]

I find this quote quite appropriate as I think of getting through security checkpoints at any airport. Those just starting to travel don't know the ropes and can get frustrated or cause delays in security lines.

---

[10]613 Funny, Inspirational and Incredibly Stupid Travel Quotes, Compiled by Darcie Conned, <http://trekity.com/travel-funinspirational-travel-quotes/> [accessed 05/19/2014].

Table 3.2 TSA and Airport Wait Time Apps and Web Sites			
Name	**Compatible Devices**	**URL**	**Price**
WhatsBusy	Desktop & Mobile	http://www.whatsbusy.com	Free
FAAwait	iOS	http://www.taclogic.com/Home.html	Free
TSA Wait Times	Web site	https://apps.tsa.dhs.gov/mytsa/wait_times_home.aspx	Free
Specific Airline Apps	Desktop & Mobile	Ex. Delta, American Airlines, etc.	Free

Experienced travelers know the tricks to speed up the process and have the timing down pat. Which are you?

The Transportation Security Administration (TSA) was hastily formed in the aftermath of 9/11. Its agents secure the nation's airports and screen both passengers and baggage to protect against terrorism and other security breaches.[11] Most travelers find that the preflight security process tedious and frustrating as it can become an obstacle to getting to their flight on time.

The TSA uses a variety of programs to screen for potential danger via technology and behavioral observation. The media and general public have highly criticized both of these techniques. Did the full body scanning kiosks violate a person's privacy? Was it really necessary to pat down a 3-year-old, especially considering the trauma it caused? Is the TSA's Screening of Passengers by Observation Technique Program (SPOT) illegal profiling? The last example has called into question whether the TSA programs are ineffective, racist, and expensive?[12] The SPOT program trains TSA agents as behavior detection officers who read body language such as facial expressions and other nonverbal clues to identity potential terrorists or dangerous individuals.

Frequent travelers often have options to deal with the TSA security clearance process. Some use web sites and apps to monitor and keep track of wait times at the security checkpoints. See Table 3.2 for a list. Others who are deemed low risk can be preapproved in Trusted Passenger Programs. See Table 3.3 for those.

---

[11]About TSA website, <http://www.tsa.gov/about-tsa> [accessed 06/09/2014].

[12]Noble V. Viewpoint: time to end profiling policies, <http://www.michigandaily.com/opinion/12viewpoint-tsa02>; December 1, 2013.

Table 3.3 TSA and Security Clearance Services		
Name	URL	Price
TSA PreCheck	http://www.tsa.gov/tsa-precheck	$85
Global Entry	http://www.cbp.gov/travel/trusted-traveler-programs/global-entry	$100
CLEAR	https://www.clearme.com	$179/year

TSA agents review a few items for each traveler—from boarding passes to IDs—to ensure you are who you are supposed to be and you are authorized to be at the airport.

IDs are a way of proving your identity. To most people, a driver's license or nondriver's license with a photo seems pretty standard. But it is not universal. The TSA does have a handy list on its web site of what IDs it will accept—although not named expressly, apparently your Facebook profile is one of them. "Zach Klein, the cofounder of Vimeo and current CEO of DIY.org, posted a message on Twitter indicating surprise that the TSA accepted his Facebook profile as proof of his identity.[13]" Why? According to TSA's web site: "We understand passengers occasionally arrive at the airport without an ID, due to lost items or inadvertently leaving them at home. Not having an ID does not necessarily mean a passenger won't be allowed to fly. If passengers are willing to provide additional information, we have other means of substantiating someone's identity, like using publicly available databases."[14]

But what if the documentation is fraudulent? Since 2002, Interpol has been compiling a database of stolen or lost passports. The database currently contains more than 40 million documents available to governments to screen.[15] The United States is one of the most prolific users of the database. However, many countries do not use it. Its underutilization came to light after news that two passengers on a missing Malaysian airliner were traveling with stolen passports.[16]

---

[13]Strange A. Why your Facebook account could be a vital travel tool, <http://mashable.com/2013/12/22/why-your-facebook-account-could-be-an-important-travel-tool/>, December 22, 2013.
[14]TSA Website. Acceptable IDs, <http://www.tsa.gov/traveler-information/acceptable-ids> [assessed 06/06/2014].
[15]Interpol Website. <http://www.interpol.int/INTERPOL-expertise/Border-management/SLTD-Database> [accessed 06/06/2014].
[16]Schmitt E. Use of stolen passports on missing jet highlights security flaw, <http://www.nytimes.com/2014/03/11/world/asia/missing-malaysian-airliner-said-to-highlight-a-security-gap.html?emc=edit_th_20140311&nl=todaysheadlines&nlid=33425801&_r=0>; March 10, 2014.

That database may be great for identifying fraudulent passports, but what about fraudulent Facebook or other social media profiles? In 2012, CNN released a report indicating that "83 million Facebook accounts are fakes and dupes."[17] Facebook estimates that "14.3 million of these accounts have been created specifically for malicious purposes—such as spamming."[18] Facebook does offer an easy way for users to report fake accounts,[19] but the numbers exceed the monitoring. Considering these numbers, it is concerning that the TSA would accept the Facebook profile on its own merit.

TSA also checks the name of passengers against the 92,000 names on its No-Fly List.[20] This number continues to increase and has raised concerns about potential discrimination against Muslims or those with Muslim names. Misidentification and duplicate names have also raised concerns as to the due process that is afforded an individual if they are identified as being on the No-Fly List.

The TSA also screens baggage—especially carry-ons. We are familiar with the 3–1–1 rule—one 3 oz. container in one small plastic bag, etc. Sometimes there are problems with what people want to take on board or what people leave behind:

- Woody's Mini-Toy Gun[21]—here was a situation in which the TSA stopped a father and confiscated a small wooden gun on a toy doll. The father sent out comments by social media. Some respondents questioned why a mini gun would pose a threat. Others wondered where the mini gun came from in the first place since the character, Woody, does not have one.
- SXSW Swag (Magazines, programs, etc.)[22]—Sometimes the ink or the advanced technology contained in printed matter can set off alarms in the TSA's sensitive screening systems.

---

[17]Kelly H. CNN, 83 million Facebook accounts are fakes and dupes, <http://www.cnn.com/2012/08/02/tech/social-media/facebook-fake-accounts/>; August 2, 2012.
[18]Ibid.
[19]Facebook Help Center. How do i report a fake account? <https://www.facebook.com/help/www/167722253287296> [accessed 06/09/2014].
[20]TSA No-Fly List. <http://www.no-fly-list.com> [accessed 06/06/2014]. When I accessed the list for this Chapter, I also search for my name—you never know?
[21]Chumley, CK, Airport security confiscates "Toy Story" Woody's mini-toy gun, <http://www.washingtontimes.com/news/2014/feb/11/airport-security-confiscates-toy-storys-woodys-mini/>; February 11, 2014.
[22]AP. SXSW swag stymies air travel, <http://www.politico.com/story/2014/03/sxsw-swag-stymies-air-travel-104613.html#ixzz2vqUIM3FN>; March 12, 2014.

- Travelers leave \$500G in change at airport security checkpoints[23]—always remember to check the little plastic bowls that you drop your change into. You never know what you may leave behind.

SECURITY BEYOND THE AIRPORTS

More than 200,000 miles of train tracks crisscross the USA without significant Federal oversight or protection[24]

Airplanes aren't the only mode of business travel. Trains, buses, and cars are also highly used, especially for local or regional travel. The reason may be because the distance to be traveled is too short to justify the high cost of an airline ticket. Another reason may be the necessity of having ready transportation (a car) for various stops or meetings along a particular route. For whatever reason, it is important to note security concerns regardless of how you travel.

As an example of how quickly risk can escalate, in February 2014 New York and New Jersey Transit police faced a new security concern as fans, tourists, and visitors overloaded the subway and metro railroad systems getting from New York to New Jersey's MetLife Stadium at the Meadowlands Sports Complex for the Super Bowl.[25] For that week, transit security was top priority along with the region's airport security.

New York's subway system has a Metro Card payment system. This is similar in various states in the United States, including the Washington, DC, area. It permits passengers to automatically purchase tickets without having to wait in long lines at the ticket counter. One of the benefits touted for the Metro Cards is that you can refill them—in terms of fees—so they can be used again and again. Questions arise as to how much information is contained on the Metro Cards and whether these cards will evolve to be connected to a more

---

[23]FoxNews. Travelers leave \$500 G in change at airport security checkpoints, <http://www.foxnews.com/politics/2013/11/30/travelers-leave-500g-in-change-at-airport-security-checkpoints/>; November 30, 2013.
[24]Parker LA. Train travelers experiencing increased security in stations, <http://www.trentonian.com/opinion/20140323/la-parker-train-travelers-experiencing-increased-security-in-stations>; March 23, 2014.
[25]Ibid.

permanent system that will contain even more information. For example, if the passenger's employer is registered with the Metro Card system to get discounts (and a pretax benefit for its employees), will the employee's "metro card" have the employer information on it? Will the coding on that card then be connected to the employee's employment status and verification like an ID card? Can the coding be hacked to enable access to the company's IT systems? Most countries keep their transportation payment systems—tokens, cards, etc.—separate. But, as the trend to integrate all financial transactions continues, this is something security and risk professionals need to monitor.

Greyhound and other bus services also conduct some security pre-screening, although not as elaborately as the airports. The bus depot is usually not as high-tech as airport terminals and depends more on local security officers than regionally or federally trained agents. This provides an opportunity for hackers to set up in a bus depot and capture information from travelers signing into their accounts from the free Wi-Fi. Secure hotspots are a necessity for any kind of travel to ensure confidentiality and to make it more difficult to steal your data.

TERMINAL SECURITY

Just as waiting in a bus depot can leave you vulnerable to a hacker attack, airport terminals can also become an obstacle course for security. Various innocent-looking traps are lying in wait to ambush the unsuspecting.

Basic safety precautions tell us to be careful when we are using an automatic teller machine (ATM) to withdraw money. But what if we are checking our bank account online?

We know to be careful to keep receipts in a safe place or discard them in a way that destroys the financial information on them. Are we as security conscious making a last-minute online purchase at our favorite retail web site?

We go for a quick bite to eat, and the restaurant offers free Wi-Fi. Do we automatically log on to check for urgent business e-mails before we board the plane? Or have we added a secure hotspot to our wireless phone service via our mobile device to add a layer of security?

What about VIP or airline lounges? Do they run on a secure network requiring a password or do they offer free public access?

SOCIAL MEDIA, TRAVEL, AND SECURITY

There is a Farmer's Insurance commercial in which the insurance professor reminds people of what they don't know. To paraphrase one of his comments: "What if you didn't know that posting a comment about your upcoming vacation on Facebook can make you more likely to have your home burglarized?"[26]

Social media allows us to share information with those we want to share with and, unfortunately, with those we do not. Many of the social media platforms also ask to include your location, acquired through the GPS in your smart device. This is how Foursquare, a social media app that permits users to check into different places, works. The object of Foursquare is to "help people keep up and meet up with friends and discover great places.[27]" It uses gamification, game mechanics, to encourage people to check into as many places as possible to earn points. Accumulate a certain number of points and you can achieve a badge or even become mayor of a certain location—earning you specific perks. Starbucks offers free coffee to Foursquare mayors of their stores. Of course, this advertises where you are at the moment of check-in, alerting those who follow you and some who don't. Make sure to check your privacy settings so your information is not public. Also, Foursquare allows you to share your check-in on other social media platforms such as Facebook and Twitter, letting even more people know your whereabouts.

One of the things I usually tell my clients is if you want to earn points on Foursquare, check in when you are leaving the location, not when you get there. Another thing to keep in mind is that Foursquare allows you to post photos of your location. Most of the time, those photos are taken with a smartphone or mobile device. The apps that run the cameras in these devices add meta-data to the photo file, such as time, date, and location. This is another way that malicious individuals can keep track of you. If they are watching you through your social media accounts, they can pick up a specific routine—including time and route—based on the geo-location information of the photos you upload. Good best practices include stripping the geo-location data from the photo before you post, do not post while you are

---

[26]You can see the commercial here, <http://www.ispot.tv/ad/7Ojv/farmers-insurance-the-more-you-know> [accessed 06/10/2014].
[27]Foursqaure About page, <https://foursquare.com/about> [accessed 06/10/2014].

traveling (wait until you return, unless you are a travel blog writer and/ or your job requires it), turn off automatic photo upload if you have a Google Plus account, and monitor who "tags" you in photos in their own accounts (which you do not control). I specifically ask my family, friends and colleagues not to tag any photo with my name (regardless of whether I am in the photo). I untag myself when they do.

Tagging brings up an important point. What shows up on social media and other online platforms about us, our company, and our work is not necessarily posted by us but by others and usually without our consent. For example, in June 2014, a tweet by the team's official sponsor leaked the passport information of the England Football Squad. According to one report: "The information was included on an official FIFA team sheet, shared with members of the press 1 h before the English team played a friendly match against Ecuador at Sun Life Stadium in Miami. Unfortunately, England's corporate sponsor, Vauxhall, clearly didn't realize that the passport numbers might be sensitive and excitedly tweeted out a smartphone photo of the line-up to ardent soccer fans."[28] Monitor what is being said about you—set up a Google alert on your name and your company name. You want to know what is being said, especially if you are not part of the conversation.

Another thing to remember—be careful about what you tweet. Joking about bombs and threats is not funny. A Dutch girl learned this the hard way. She was arrested after tweeting a threat against American Airlines.[29] She immediately and profusely apologized after sending the tweet, but American Airlines took it very seriously. Millions of dollars and hours of time can be wasted evacuating an airport, investigating the potential threat, delaying planes and thousands of passengers, etc. Apparently the Secret Service wants to find a way to distinguish between jokes, sarcasm, and real threats and have supposedly issued a request for software to detect the difference to prevent waste of resources.[30] Stay tuned to see if they succeed.

---

[28]Cluley G. England footballers have their passport details leaked on Twitter, <http://www.welivesecurity.com/2014/06/04/england-footballers-passport-details-leaked-twitter/>; June 4, 2014.
[29]Maxon T. Dutch girl arrested after tweeting threat against American Airlines, <http://aviation-blog.dallasnews.com/2014/04/reports-dutch-girl-arrested-after-tweeting-threat-against-american-airlines.html/>; April 14, 2014.
[30]Kollmeyer B. Are you kidding? Secret Service hunts for sarcasm-detecting software, <http://blogs.marketwatch.com/themargin/2014/06/04/are-you-kidding-secret-service-hunts-for-sarcasm-detecting-software/>; June 4, 2014.

DURING THE FLIGHT SECURITY

I travel light. But not at the same speed.
—Jarod Kintz[31]

Can you sleep on a plane? If not, how do you pass the time? There was a time when you could not turn on your laptop or digital devices while in the air. This has changed. Today many airlines offer an in-flight Internet connection—at a cost, of course. Part of the cost doesn't involve money; it involves the opportunity for a security breach. Do you have to take advantage of in-flight Internet for business reasons or can you afford to be Internet-Free in the sky?

A good rule of thumb is if you do not need to get online during your flight, do not. Someone with bad intentions may be watching you and where you put your equipment. Your decision can also depend on the cabin you are sitting in. However, does First Class automatically mean better security than Coach? Do you remember special screen attachments called privacy screens to prevent those near you from spying on your computer as you work? Shoulder surfing exists now more than ever. Also, do not leave laptops or mobile devices on your seat unattended when you go to the restroom or walk about the cabin to stretch your legs. They become accessible to anyone who may pass by (snoops, light-fingered thieves).

TRAVEL STRESS AND SECURITY

Travel can be stressful, and you have already endured quite a bit just getting to your seat. Time to sit back and relax, right? There are two great reasons for getting some rest—so you can be alert and prepared when you arrive for your meeting but also so you can be alert and prepared regarding security and safety.

How important is sleep and relaxation during travel? Enough to encourage airlines to take notice and offer some high-sleep amenities. Dr. Russel A. Sanna, Executive Director of Harvard Medical School's division of sleep medicine, states that there are three pillars of health—diet, exercise, and sleep.[32] Two airlines taking this to heart are Etihad Airways and Delta Air Lines. Etihad Airways—after almost 2 years of

---

[31]Kintz J. The days of yay are here! Wake me up when they're over, 2011.
[32]Rosenbloom S. New York Times, The quest for sweet dreams, <http://www.nytimes.com/2014/03/30/travel/from-airlines-to-hotels-a-quest-to-help-you-sleep.html>; March 26, 2014.

research with the American Center for Psychiatry and Neurology in Abu Dhabi—introduced a sleep program that includes all-natural mattresses, mood lighting, noise-canceling headphones, pillow mist, and calming pulse-point oil.[33] Delta Air Lines now offers Westin Heavenly bedding products (pillow and comforters) in BusinessElite International and some domestic flights[34] as well as a white-noise channel on Delta Radio.

Our mobile devices can be sleep stealers. Every time we hear a chime indicating a text message, phone call, or e-mail, how many can resist immediately answering it? Or, if we wake up suddenly do we automatically reach for our smartphone and immediately become awake because of the blue light emanating from the palm-sized device?

Trains and buses also acknowledge the importance of sleep, considering that they take longer than airplanes to reach the same destination. Amtrak has the Viewliner and Superliner Sleeping Car with three types of bedrooms: Standard, Deluxe, and Accessible Bedrooms.[35] As for overnight bus travel, must-haves include earplugs, eye masks, and neck pillows.[36]

If you can't sleep while traveling, the key is to relax—so meditation may do the trick. Table 3.4 offers some sleep and meditation apps (of the hundreds out there) that you can use on your next trip.

AIRPORT AND TRAVEL GAME APPS

Airline travel is hours of boredom interrupted by moments of stark terror.
—Al Boliska[37]

Can't sleep and don't want to do work? Games may be the thing for you. Airlines may have a game console available (with games for free or for purchase). Or, you may want to play one of your own.

---

[33]Rosenbloom S. New York Times, The quest for sweet dreams, <http://www.nytimes.com/2014/03/30/travel/from-airlines-to-hotels-a-quest-to-help-you-sleep.html>; March 26, 2014.

[34]Delta Press Release. Delta Air Lines to offer Westin Heavenly In-Flight Bedding in Busineselite, <http://news.delta.com/index.php?s=20295&item=124217>; February 26, 2013.

[35]Amtrak Sleeping Cars, <http://www.amtrak.com/sleeping-car-virtual-tours> [accessed 06/04/2014]. For true sleeping opulence on the rails see Jordan R. Travel + Leisure Magazine, World's Fanciest Sleeper Cars, <http://www.travelandleisure.com/articles/worlds-fanciest-sleeper-cars>; July, 2012.

[36]The Planet D. Night bus travel: 11 tips for safety, survival and sleep, <http://theplanetd.com/night-bus-travel-11-tips-for-safety-survival-and-sleep/>; August 31, 2013.

[37]613 Funny, Inspirational and Incredibly Stupid Travel Quotes, Compiled by Darcie Conned, <http://trekity.com/travel-funinspirational-travel-quotes/> [accessed 05/19/2014].

Table 3.4 Sleep and Meditation Apps			
Name	Compatible Devices	URL	Price
Sleep Genius	iOS & Android	http://sleepgenius.com	Free/$5 upgrade
Sleep Pillow	iPhone, iPad	https://itunes.apple.com/us/app/sleep-pillow-sounds-white/id410351918?mt=8	$1.99
Sleepbot	iOS & Android	http://mysleepbot.com	Free
Sleep Cycle Alarm Clock	iPhone	http://www.sleepcycle.com	$0.99
Deep Sleep with Andrew Johnson	iOS & Android	https://itunes.apple.com/us/app/deep-sleep-andrew-johnson/id337349999?mt=8	$2.99
Pzizz Sleep	iPhone	http://pzizz.com	$4.99
Relax & Rest Guided Meditations	iOS & Android	http://www.meditationoasis.com	$0.99
Relaxing Nature Sounds	iPhone	http://rtstudio.net/NatureScenes.html	$1.99

Table 3.5 Airport and Travel Game Apps			
Name	Compatible Devices	URL	Price
Airport City	iOS & Android	http://www.gameairportcity.com	Free
Airport Madness Challenge	iPhone, iPad	http://fluik.com/airport-madness-challenge/	Free
Flight Control	iOS & Android	http://www.firemonkeys.com.au/#	$0.99/ $4.99
RC Flight Simulator	iOS	http://happybytesapps.com	Free
Traveler's Quest	iOS	http://kittycode.com/products/travelersquest/	Free

Keep in mind all of the security concerns regarding online activity and how much information you actually have to give out in order to play that free game as well as the financial information from your credit card you are using to purchase the game. Table 3.5 lists some for you.

As we come to the end of this chapter, I leave you with a rundown of some very funny travel tweets and a Pre-Departure and Departure Checklist. As you laugh a little and release some of the travel stress, it will prepare you for Chapter 4 and the security concerns regarding arrival and duration at your destination. Just exactly who knows you're coming?

100 Ridiculously Funny Travel Tweets, November 11, 2013, Traveler's Lagniappe Blog http://shipsandtripstravel.com/lagniappe/100-ridiculously-funny-travel-tweets-deserve-retweet/.

●●●──────────────────────────────────────

Checklist: Predeparture and Departure

- Apply online or in person for required international travel documentation.
  - Passport, visas, international driver's permit, etc.
- Pack with security in mind.
  - Take only those devices and data that you really, really need.
- Contact cellular service provider.
- Inform company IT about your travel for extra safety and security precautions.
  - Prepare devices for secured travel.
    - Update antivirus software.
    - Encrypt your data.
- Secure office for while you are away and set up assistant access to devices and data.
- Prepare for financial transactions abroad.
  - Contact bank or other financial institution to let them know you will be overseas and for how long.
  - Inquire whether the company has its own financial credit card for business travel.
  - Set up a separate credit card for the particular business travel.
- Prepare for TSA and other transport security procedures.
- Acquire and set up a secured hotspot for Internet service.
- Be cautious of social media and online activity.
  - Monitor social media while you are away.
- Relax during the flight, but stay alert regarding security and your electronic devices.

CHAPTER 4

Arrival and Duration

Where you come from does matter—but not nearly as much as where you are headed.

—Jodi Picoult[1]

This chapter focuses on what happens at the destination. We will discuss those pesky customs officers, the very real threat of corruption that can lead to confiscated technology, nefarious fees, security risks relating to online currency acquisition, and in-country transportation. We will also discuss security for you, your technology, and your data and how to protect your various personal health and medical management apps, Wi-Fi security awareness in foreign states and hotels, Tripit, online censorship laws, and other critical issues.

---

[1]Goodreads Travel Quotations. <http://www.goodreads.com/quotes/tag/travel?page=2> [accessed 06/08/2014].

ARRIVALS, CUSTOMS, BORDER CROSSINGS

Arriving at your destination may be a relief or may cause anxiety depending on whether you have been there before (and not too much time has passed since your last visit) and why you are there now. Frequency and repetitiveness breed familiarity, which increases our confidence level because we know more or less what to expect and can prepare accordingly. However, if you travel frequently you know that things may not always stay the same. Economic, political, and geo-political events may affect travel in and out of the country as well as travel and business dealings within it. New security procedures may be in place for foreign arrivals and/or new attitudes exhibited toward foreign travelers—such as heightened suspicion. The preparation work you did on reviewing the latest intelligence and news about the country will be very helpful at this point. As your plane is landing, review on your notepad, tablet, or even smartphone your notes so you will be ready for what comes next.

Some customs locations and border crossings are more difficult than others. Consider, for example, if you are arriving in a country under an authoritarian regime or a location where high corruption is the norm. During an inspection (i.e., search) of your belongings, be prepared to answer a few questions regarding your digital equipment. Some examples:

1. Is your equipment for your personal/business use or are you importing it for someone else? If you cannot prove to the official's satisfaction that you are not importing the equipment, be prepared to potentially pay a high duty, tax, or fee.
2. Is the data your equipment contains of a national security concern? You may be asked to unlock your laptop and even decrypt the data (if encrypted) for the official to browse through your files. If determined to be of security interest, your equipment may be confiscated or impounded, leaving you and your company liable for data breach, deemed exports of technological know-how, client confidentiality violations, loss of property, etc.
3. What is the purpose of your visit? When the purpose is business and it is combined with the other two previous questions, suspicion may be greater than normal.
4. How long are you staying and where else are you traveling to or from? These questions continue the inquiry into the purpose of your visit and address any national security concerns the officials may have.

It is important during these inspections, searches, questioning sessions, that you be patient and not do anything that would arouse more suspicion. If you are traveling with someone from the country or have a country host who is assisting you in the arrival process, follow their lead and let them do the talking in the native language if possible. Some clients at the destination country may have certain authority or influence to make the process of entering the country less difficult or to bypass it all together. When setting logistics for the travel, it is good to ask your host if they know of any arrival and security challenges and if they can be of assistance should a problem occur.

DESTINATION TRANSPORTATION AND SECURITY

You can't understand a city without using its public transportation system.
—Erol Ozan[2]

Leaving the transportation terminal and traveling within the destination country involve a number of considerations, from personal safety to language to data security. As Graham Cluley, senior technology consultant at security specialist Sophos, stated: "Clearly the risk is not the cost of replacing a stolen laptop or Blackberry mislaid in the back of a Bangkok taxi. The primary danger is that cybercriminals will be able to access confidential, sensitive information that could be of value to them, be that a laptop containing personal information that could be exploited by identity thieves, sensitive company data, a vector into your corporate network, or usernames and passwords that could lead to corporate espionage. Even a corporate address book will have contact details of your employees, customers, and partners that could be exploited in a spear-phishing or targeted malware attack.[3]"

His words are a reminder of what is truly at stake in our digital world and what has value in our digital economy as we carry sensitive data with us. Taxis are only one way of getting around. Buses, trains, tuk-tuks, canal boats, and more offer options to get from one place to another as well as potential venues for losing our devices and data.

[2]Ibid.
[3]Computer Weekly. Top five data security travel issues: Protect sensitive information on business trips,   <http://www.computerweekly.com/feature/Top-five-data-security-travel-issues-Protect-sensitive-information-on-business-trips>; October, 2009.

In some locations, rental vehicles may be the best option. If this is your alternative, consider the following factors:

1. Insurance—Is this an umbrella program offered by your company or does it come from the rental agency? There may be different levels of coverage offered by the insurance. Make sure to select the one that offers appropriate coverage for the duration of the rental period.
2. Driver(s)—Does the company policy indicate who can drive a rental vehicle based on prior driving records or requirements? For example, do you need to have a valid international driver's permit in addition to a current state-issued driver's license. Are you required to have a pretty-clean Department of Motor Vehicles (DMV) driving history without any major transgressions? These issues bring up two considerations for employers: on the one hand, are you intruding into the employee's privacy requiring disclosure of a driving history? On the other hand, is the company making itself liable in certain scenarios, such as a car crash, because it should have known the employee was a bad driver who would put others at risk?
3. Other passengers—Does the company policy address the issue of other passengers, nonemployees, in the rental vehicle and liability toward them?
4. Fuel and other—Does the company policy address any of the additional requirements of driving rental vehicles including fuel, oil, parking expenses, and repairs?

HOTELS AND SECURITY

Business center and kiosk PCs are like petri dishes full of bacteria.
—Kenneth van Wyk[4]

There are two levels of security to consider regarding hotels and lodging. The first is the hotel operator—a bird's eye view to ensure the safety and security of all their guests. The second is the guest, a much more subjective view of personal safety and security. Both levels are important and work together. When the hotel operator does its security function well, it means the guest's efforts are doubly rewarded.

[4]Van Wyk K. Enjoy your trip, but protect the data you take with you, <http://bit.ly/1irwrOV>; December 2, 2013.

During the logistics and planning phase of business travel, your company may or may not take into consideration security rankings and controls of certain hotels. Security Magazine does an annual security ranking of the top 500 companies in various industries in the United States. Hotels are listed under the hospitality/casino category.[5] There is not a global security-ranking equivalent, although international hotel security management is a very hot topic in terms of reports, articles, and hospitality conferences. The US Department of State Overseas Advisory Council (OSAC) has a great hotel security checklist that can be used to make a security assessment for any hotel or lodging. You can find it at http://1.usa.gov/1pBdCwZ. Not only can your company use it for planning, but you can also use it once you get to your hotel.

As more and more data breaches make headlines, travelers are becoming increasingly wary of security risks. The hospitality industry is taking note. Many hospitality companies are looking at technology to enhance the guest experience and provide additional security. For example, surveillance cameras are becoming smaller and more powerful, offering high definition images and real-time streaming to tablets and smartphones. Hotels are using security self-checklists and other tools to assess their security preparation. Hotels are also posting security certificates or assessments online for guest access (see Table 4.1).

Hotel key cards are becoming smarter with Radio Frequency Identification (RFID) technology. Assa Abloy and Starwood Hotels are testing mobile key solutions, having guests download an app and use it to enter their hotel rooms. Other hotels, such as the Marriott Marquis, are taking an additional step and offering mobile check-in

Table 4.1 Hotel Security Apps			
Name	**Compatible Devices**	**URL**	**Price**
Safety & Security Self-Inspection Checklist	iOS, Android, Blackberry, Windows	http://www.gocanvas.com/mobile-forms-apps/8841-Safety-Security-Self-Inspection-Checklist-for-Hotels#	Free 30-day trial
SmartGuest	iOS, Android, Blackberry, Windows	http://enterprise.alcatel-lucent.com/?event=HITEC&page=LosAngeles_2014	Customized

[5]Security Magazine. Security Magazine's 2013 security 500 ranking, <http://www.securitymagazine.com/articles/84860-security-rankings>; November 5, 2013.

and check-out that allow guests to bypass the registration desk and go straight to their room.[6] Many hotels are using hotel-brand-specific apps to provide just-in-time updates about room status, restaurant menus, and other relevant guest information.

Although most travelers consider self-service check-in convenient, it is a security concern. Hotel management doesn't have a visual account of who comes onto hotel premises. The hotel staff is usually trained to make eye contact with guests and others in the hotel to keep track of any unidentified or suspicious individuals. If the guests bypass the front desk, other controls need to be in place to address this security concern. For example, will the new apps have facial recognition or another biometric identification protocol? If so, could that be considered an invasion of privacy? Does the security benefit outweigh privacy rights since guests get convenience?

WI-FI AND PUBLIC COMPUTERS

We have been warned about the security risks of using public unsecured Wi-Fi networks to connect to the Internet and access data. However, that doesn't seem to stop many of us. Consider a 2013 survey commissioned by Mountain View, California-based security software company AnchorFree and conducted by travel research firm PhoCusWright. This survey questioned 2203 American travelers who took at least one trip of more than 75 miles in the previous 12 months. According to SC Magazine, "although the results indicate that four out of five respondents felt their personal information was not safe when on a public Wi-Fi network, nearly 84% do not take action to ensure their data is secure, according to the study, which establishes that eight out of ten travelers use public Wi-Fi on their trips."[7]

Hotels sometimes offer a business center with computers for their guests. Sometimes these are open to the public. It is best to steer clear of them, as they are not secure. If you use them, check only

---

[6]It is important to note that apps are not available in all locations. Restrictions do apply especially in some countries. The Marriott web site has the following disclaimer: Regulations in Armenia, France, Italy, Kazakhstan, Portugal, Poland, Russia, Spain, and Turkey allow for mobile check-in but require guests to check out with the front desk. Mobile check-in and check-out are not available in Japan. <http://www.marriott.com/marriott/mobile-check-in-marriott-hotels-and-resorts.mi> [accessed 06/25/2014].

[7]Israeli Homeland Security (iHLS). Most U.S. travelers are careless while using public Wi-Fi, <http://bit.ly/1mM8tyW>; December 1, 2013.

nonimportant information and do not download anything from them. Also, keep in mind that strange flash drives or USB sticks can be potential sources of infection, even when they are loaned to you with the best intentions.

DURATION AND DATA SECURITY

While you are in the destination country, adhering to security best practices regarding your data should be the norm. Some tips to keep your data secure while away from home base include:

- Remember Heartbleed—this bug made us aware that the Secure Sockets Layer (SSL) as in "https:" is not enough.
- Use virtual private networks (VPN) connections whenever possible.
- Consider getting a country SIM card for your tablet computer or mobile phone.
- Clear your browser after every use (delete history files, caches, cookies, URL, and temporary Internet files).
- Don't connect your flash drives to strange devices.
- Avoid using the "Remember me" feature on web sites and never for passwords.
- Turn off the computer when you are not using it; sleeping is not the same as off.
- Keep your devices in padding or specialized outer protection (like Otterbox, etc.).
- Make sure to have noted someone the exact make, model, and serial or service numbers of your laptop, tablet, and/ or other devices you have with you (mini inventory).
- Don't let others use your laptop or other devices.

DURATION AND APPS

A number of apps are available to assist you in navigating the everyday functions of being in a new location: maps, currency exchange, time zones, etc. Table 4.2 lists some Travel Productivity Apps you can review. Even if the apps are listed for iOS, keep in mind that you can find compatible apps for Android, Blackberry, Windows, and Google. Keep in mind, too, any company policies regarding mobile use and app downloads. For example, your company may have blacklisted certain apps the IT department has identified as containing malware.

Table 4.2 Travel Productivity Apps			
Name	Compatible Devices	URL	Price
Word Lens	iOS, Android, Google Glass	http://questvisual.com	$4.99/language pair
iTranslate	iPhone, iPad	http://www.itranslateapp.com	Free
Ask Ziggy	iOS, Android, Windows	http://www.ask-ziggy.com	Free
World Clock Pro	iPhone, iPad	http://www.thealarmclockcompany.com	$1.99
Currency App	iOS & Android	http://currencyapp.com	Free
Commandr Compass	iOS	http://happymagenta.com/compass/	$3.99
Google Earth	iOS & Android	http://www.google.com/earth/explore/products/mobile.html	Free
Mapquest Mobile	iOS, Android, Windows, Amazon	http://mobile.mapquest.com/#intro	Free
Waze	iOS, Android, Windows	https://www.waze.com	Free

Or, your company may have its own corporate app store from which you can download specific approved apps. One other item to highlight is leading-edge technology. Be careful. Most countries have more stringent privacy laws than the United States and are still working out how to deal with wearable technology such as Google Glass.

DURATION AND HEALTH

When you travel, remember a foreign country is not designed to make you comfortable. It is designed to makes its own people comfortable.
—Clifton Fadiman[8]

What made colonization of the Americas possible in the late 1400s and early 1500s? Smallpox.[9] Back then the disease was carried on sailing vessels that took months to reach their destination. Today, air travelers can spread disease between two countries thousands of miles apart in a matter of hours. Travel technology also means that we can *go to* a disease faster than ever before by simply landing in an affected area.

---

[8] <http://www.goodreads.com/quotes/tag/travel?page=2> [accessed 06/08/2014].
[9] PBS. Guns, Germs and steel, <http://www.pbs.org/gunsgermssteel/variables/smallpox.html> [accessed 06/26/2014].

International SOS, a world-leading medical and travel security risk services company, conducted a study in 2013 to assess the health risks associated with certain travel regions. The study found that "the data from approximately 600,000 medical cases in 2013 revealed that over 40% of medical cases occurred in countries (Asia and Middle East) classed as 'high' or 'extreme' risk, a sharp increase from less than 25% in 2010. 11 percent were due to infectious illnesses including malaria and dengue fever. In medical terms, Europe remained a largely low risk continent, while medical cases by risk category in the Americas were generally at similar levels to 2010."[10]

Recent outbreaks of the severe acute respiratory syndrome (SARS) virus in 2003, the Avian Bird Flu that spread throughout Asia in 2004 and, more recently, the H1N1 swine flu pandemic of 2009, highlight the potential for the quick spread of disease through air travel.

Making the right health preparation before traveling is important. Once in the destination country, however, ensure you have any medical and health-care-related information readily available. These can be organized on your mobile device or an app connected to a larger traveler care program.

Another health-related issue to consider is the possibility of being hurt while on a trip. Most companies have worker's compensation for on-the-job injuries, but when you are traveling overseas are you on the job 24/7? It's important to check your company's policy and reporting procedures to know if they specify any nuances. For example, is an employee on the job when he or she is at dinner with clients? The answer, probably, is yes. Is an employee on the job if he or she has dinner in their hotel room? Maybe. Do after-hour activities with or without a client count as being on the job? What if alcohol or drugs are involved?[11] Your company's policies should be readily accessible via your mobile device.

---

[10]Ani. India among "high risk" countries for business travelers, <http://www.business-standard.com/article/news-ani/india-among-high-risk-countries-for-business-travelers-114022500584_1.html> February 25, 2014.

[11]Felzke H. Risk management: employee business travel and liability, <http://www.rentalmanagementmag.com/Article/tabid/670/smid/1276/ArticleID/20458/reftab/685/t/Default.aspx>; April 2, 2014.

DURATION AND STAYING LEGAL

Being detained or jailed overseas, or having one of your relatives or friends arrested and in prison overseas, can be very traumatic, distressing and frightening. Prison conditions in many countries can be significantly harsher.[12]

The preceding quote is from the Australian government. It could, though, be from a variety of other sovereign governments. Many countries caution their citizens who travel abroad to obey local laws. The first step in doing that is to become knowledgeable or at least aware of what some of these laws may be and how they may affect you and your business travel. Keep in mind that most countries have standard internationally recognized laws criminalizing certain illegal activity such as theft, murder. But there are interesting nuances. Yahoo Travel has compiled a list of "Weird Laws" to know before you travel.[13] They include what to wear and not to wear in certain places like Vatican City, no chewing gum in Thailand, no swearing in Queensland, Australia, and not flushing a public toilet in Singapore can cost you over $500 (USD). Below you will find examples of two traditional areas of laws related to travel and online.

Anti-Bribery and Anti-Corruption

One great resource is Latham & Watkins, LLP's AB&C Laws™ app— an easily accessible guide to anti-bribery and anti-corruption legislation in 13 major economies in Asia, the Middle East, Europe, and the United States. It covers key topics of offences, territorial application, legislative framework, limitation, penalties, and official guidance.[14] You may think 13 is a small number, but it covers the most common destinations.

Social Media and Government Censorship

- China—Facebook is prohibited. In addition, the Chinese government passed a law in September 2013 that if an individual "posts a message online that the government deems defamatory or false and if it receives more than 500 retweets (or shares) or 5000 views

[12]Australia Government. Smart Traveler Information Website, <http://www.smartraveller.gov.au/tips/arrest-jail.html> [accessed 06/26/2014].

[13]O'Mara K. Yahoo travel: weird laws to know before you travel, <https://travel.yahoo.com/ideas/weird-laws-to-know-before-you-travel.html>; June 20, 2012.

[14]Latham, Watkins. LLP mobile apps page, <http://www.lw.com/mobileApps> [accessed 06/11/2014].

then the person responsible for the post could receive up to 3 years in jail."

- Vietnam—The Vietnamese government passed Decree 72 which makes it a criminal offence to share news articles or information gathered from government sites over online blogs and social media sites.

- Burma—The Electronic Transactions Law 2004 allows imprisonment of up to 15 years for "acts by using electronic transactions technology" deemed "detrimental to the security of the State or prevalence of law and order or community peace and tranquility or national solidarity or national economy or national culture." So a person can serve a hefty jail sentence for being on the receiving end of an e-mail the government isn't so fond of.

THE TRAVELER TRACKED

Everywhere I go, I'm second to arrive. My reputation precedes me, and sometimes it skips out on the bill.

—Jarod Kintz[15]

Letting someone know where you are can be good (personal safety, emergency rescue) or bad (think surveillance, stalking, espionage). Sometimes it is a choice we make—for example, using Foursquare to check into a place using our smartphone's GPS to gather points and/or other online perks or directly posting our location and actions to Facebook. Other times, our whereabouts is discreetly contained in the metadata of items we post online—like the geo-tag of a photograph taken with our smartphone. Then there are those incidents where we had no control over who knows where we are. That kind of tracking may be for research purposes. For example, Chinese Internet giant Baidu tracked the travel rush during the Spring Festival or Chinese New Year holiday through its mapping service. This led to concerns from some users that their privacy has been invaded.[16]

Another positive use of tracking is with certain travel assistance and personal security apps. International SOS has a Travel Assistance App

---

[15]Kintz J. At even one penny, this book would be overpriced. In fact, free is too expensive, because you'd still waste time by reading it; 2012.
[16]Want China Times. Baidu's Spring Festival travel tracker prompts privacy concerns, <http://www.wantchinatimes.com/news-subclass-cnt.aspx?id=20140215000054&cid=1103>;   February 15, 2014.

with location check-in that works in conjunction with its SOS TravelTracker platform.[17] It works on iOS, Android, Blackberry, and is free for SOS members. Rich Gallagher, International SOS Chief Digital Officer, describes the apps' advantage: "Imagine a traveler flying abroad. Using travel booking data their employer easily knows where the traveler's plane is due to land. But what if upon landing, the traveler takes a 150 km taxi ride to a remote work site? With one click, that traveler has the ability to confirm where they are located at that time, with their location details clearly visible on their employer's TravelTracker map."[18]

Another traveler tracker and disaster recovery app is i-Care app[19] by TMC Inntel. This app underpins the duty of care employers owe employees. Both of these apps, as well as others, rely on employees, who may have their own reasons for turning devices off at certain times and some venues, to activate and use them correctly so they can track their whereabouts. Training about why these apps are important for personal safety and security is critical in getting employee buy-in.

Not all tracking is benign. There have been a number of reports of foreign governments spying on foreign travelers,[20] especially if the traveler is an executive, senior government official, or otherwise noteworthy target. All business travelers should be aware, even if they are not at the executive level, that there are a number of "threat actors abroad: delivering malicious code to electronic devices; accessing the device to track their location; activating the microphone on a smartphone to eavesdrop; and intercepting voice and data communications sent electronically."[21]

[17]SOS App Page. <http://app.lk/sos-member> [accessed May, 2014].
[18]Koumelis T. New assistance app from international SOS: for safer, smarter business travel in 2014, <http://www.traveldailynews.com/news/article/59296/new-assistance-app-from-international>; February 28, 2014.
[19]Chetwynd C. Analysis: keeping travelers safe, <http://buyingbusinesstravel.com/feature/3021725-analysis-keeping-travellers-safe>; November 30, 2013.
[20]Fekete J. Postmedia News. Foreign governments spying on travelling Canadian diplomats, PM's security adviser warns in secret memo, <http://news.nationalpost.com/2014/05/22/foreign-governments-spying-on-travelling-canadian-diplomats-harpers-security-adviser-warns-in-secret-memo/>; May 22, 2014.
[21]Fekete J. Foreign governments spying on travelling Canadian diplomats, PM's security adviser warns in secret memo, <http://news.nationalpost.com/2014/05/22/foreign-governments-spying-on-travelling-canadian-diplomats-harpers-security-adviser-warns-in-secret-memo/>; May 22, 2014.

VIRTUAL KIDNAPPING

No one could believe that a jetliner could simply vanish, but that is exactly what happened with Malaysian Airlines Flight MH370 in early 2014. As of the writing of this book, the plane still has not been found. Perhaps an update to this book will provide factual answers. The plane's disappearance reminds us that technology—even tracking technology—is not infallible. Although we may feel constantly connected at home with our mobile devices, they do not always work overseas. We are all familiar with cellular dead zones where service has not been installed or your provider does not offer coverage. There are also times that you may venture to a remote location such as the mountains. Phones run out of battery, or you just may want to turn yours off and tune out.

The factors above have led to a recent trend in virtual kidnappings. A phone call is made demanding ransom, but the "victim" was not physically kidnapped.[22] How do you determine whether a reported kidnapping was real when there is spotty cell phone reception or no way to connect with the person who allegedly was abducted? In 2008, Mexico created a hotline for victims of virtual extortion. In 2009, "CBS News reported that the hotline setup in Mexico City to deal with extortion cases had received 44,000 calls since December. The hotline statistics recorded were 22,851 extortion attempts avoided, 3415 telephone numbers identified as being tied to extortionists, and 1627 people who paid off the virtual kidnappers."[23]

Even though the kidnapping may not be real, the tactic exploits real fears, especially of those close to the alleged victim.[24] Three best practices in terms of this security risk are:

1. Establish a code word to verify kidnapping claims. This can be done officially with the company, unofficially with family members, or both since potential virtual kidnappers may call your company or significant other.

---

[22]Gillingham F. Virtual kidnapping: advice on how to handle a widespread scam, <http://www.healthytravelblog.com/2010/04/14/virtual-kidnapping-advice-on-how-to-handle-a-widespread-scam/>; April 14, 2010.
[23]Lippert C. Virtual kidnappings: on the rise, <http://www.cbsnews.com/news/virtual-kidnappings-on-the-rise/>; April 30, 2008.
[24]Lacey M. Exploiting real fears with "Virtual Kidnappings", <http://www.nytimes.com/2008/04/29/world/americas/29mexico.html?partner=rssnyt&emc=rss>; April 29, 2008.

2. Listen and learn about this potential scam. There is a great FBI podcast interviewing Mollie Halpern and Tony Robleto regarding the state of virtual kidnappings up to 2014. http://www.fbi.gov/news/podcasts/thisweek/virtual-kidnappings.mp3/view

3. If your company sends executives or other employees to high-risk areas, consider purchasing kidnap and ransom insurance. Ensure that the insurance is comprehensive and will cover: kidnap and alleged kidnap, extortion, wrongful detention, and hijacking.

SECURITY APPS FOR WOMEN TRAVELERS

"Sarai Sierra—This was not a case of wrong place, wrong time. She was not engaged in risky behavior. This is a terrifying case of what can—and does—happen to female travelers abroad.[25]"

Why do I need to write a special section regarding security and women travelers? Even after all the years I have traveled internationally, there are still places I would not venture alone. I say this not just because of reports of violence against women and kidnappings of women travelers, but also because of my own experiences of not feeling safe in certain countries I have visited. Reality makes this section necessary, although I am well aware many women are fearless and will construe my concerns as sexist.

Security is also about awareness of bad things that may happen and why they may happen. We need to understand that there is a truth regarding violence against women around the world—due to religious or cultural beliefs based on fashion (length of skirt), coverage (or amount of skin shown), time when a woman can roam (not at night), numbers traveling (not alone), where (even resorts), and how women get around (only reliable taxis from the hotel).[26]

It is especially important that women be aware of what is going on around them. Do not make a call or use your smartphone to access the Internet as you are walking down a street or traveling to your location. It can wait. Your distraction can make you an easy target for theft of your laptop (and data) or physical harm. In some countries,

---

[25]Wolfe L. New York Times. Women alert to travel's darker side, <http://nyti.ms/1s8yroT>; May 23, 2014.
[26]Ibid.

Name	Compatible Devices	URL	Price
Table 4.3 Mobile Security Apps for Women Travelers			
GoSuraksheit	iOS & Android	https://itunes.apple.com/tc/app/go-suraksheit/id724254561?mt = 8	Free
		Enables you to seek help from the contacts you trust the most from almost anywhere.	
Nirbhaya SOS—Be Fearless	iOS, Android & Windows	http://smartcloudtek.com	$0.99
		An app that can be used in any type of emergency to protect women, children, and your near and dear ones using a "Single" click Distress signal.	
YWCA Safety Alert	iOS & Android	http://bit.ly/1l4KnUy	Free
		A simple tap on the alert button or a shake of the phone in an emergency situation activates an alarm, which gives off a loud shrilling sound to attract the attention of passers-by within the vicinity. A discrete distress signal for help will also be sent to the user's preset list of emergency contacts via a preprogrammed e-mail message.	
iFollow	Android	http://ifollow.aucupa.com	Free
		iFollow will get activated when shaking the device for 5 s and app will automatically dial a voice call to your prime contact configured in the device.	
Circle of 6	iOS & Android	https://www.facebook.com/Circleof6	Free
		Designed to help prevent sexual abuse.	
Hollabak	iOS & Android	http://www.ihollaback.org	Free
		Help end street harassment one hollaback at a time as you catch those creeps in the act and submit your story to be recorded and mapped on ihollback.org.	
bSafe	iOS, Andorid & Blackberry	http://getbsafe.com	Free
		Personal safety app.	
Guardly	iOS, Android, Blackberry, Windows	https://www.guardly.com/technology/mobile-safety-apps/	Free, $1.99 month, $19.99 year
		This app places a phone call to your contacts with your name, exact location, and the type of emergency.	

gender-specific transportation is available. For example, Mexico City has women-only buses, and India has begun a program of certain train cars being designated as female-only. Even Dubai has instituted "pink taxis" for women-only transportation.[27] Some oppose these measures

[27]Kirk M. The gray area in "Pink" transportation, <http://www.citylab.com/commute/2014/05/gray-area-pink-transportation/9030/>; May 5, 2014.

as being too one-sided or not enough. Others see these experiments as a start to deal with the issue of women safety.

Regardless of your gender and where you stand on women's rights, acknowledging that other countries' values and beliefs in this area may not be aligned with yours is a good best practice. Another one is to review the list of mobile security apps for women travelers in Table 4.3. You can never be too safe.

Checklist: Arrival and Duration

- Before departing the plane check to make sure you have all of your belongings: carry-ons, digital devices, etc.
  - Turn off the Wi-Fi function so the device does not automatically connect to an unsecured public network in the airport.
- Before departing the plane check your itinerary for connecting flights or next destination (ground transportation, business meeting, client office, hotel, etc.).
  - Check the airport terminal's map (it can be found in the in-flight magazine, online or via an app) to know how to get to where you need to go.
- Have any required documentation ready to show for passport inspection, visa acquisition, customs, etc. but do not hold it or have the information displayed for anyone to see.
  - Some countries require you to get your visa when you arrive in the country.
  - Follow the lines and remember to be patient. Do not jump ahead or cut in front of anyone. You do not want to make yourself conspicuous.
- Comply with instructions given by a customs or border official regarding digital equipment.
  - Keep note of the when, where, and who is doing the asking so if your device gets confiscated or damaged you have the information required for insurance and reporting purposes.
- Limit the use of any public Wi-Fi available in the hotel lobby, hotel room, offices you may visit, or other meeting spaces.
  - Beware of "evil twin" hotel networks.
  - Use secured, password-protected networks or a secured personal hub provided by your wireless provider.
- Place all digital devices in a secured location if you are not taking them with you (e.g., if you are going to a dinner function).
  - Keep data drives separate from the laptop or tablet.
  - Not all hotel room safes are "safe."

- Be aware of your surroundings and people who may be "coincidently" showing up wherever you show up. They may be following you.
  - Check on any kidnap/ransom policies and/or insurance your company may have.
  - Set up "kidnap" code to verify kidnapping.
- Monitor your health and the general health of the destination area.
- Learn about local laws that may affect you and the purpose of your business travel.
- Be careful of what you post to social media sites regarding your location and travel plans.
  - Remove geo-tagging from any photos you upload online.

CHAPTER 5

Return to Home Base

Arrival in the world is really a departure and that, which we call departure, is only a return.[1]

This chapter explores the security risks involved when you return to your home base or office. The key is to ensure that no IT viruses or other malware traveled back with you, etc. and that any data you took with you has safely returned with you without any unauthorized access or other breach.

[1]Stojanovic D. The Sun watches the Sun; 2012.

GETTING TO THE AIRPORT ON TIME

How did it get so late so soon?
—Dr. Seuss[2]

All tips in regards to personal safety and data security relating to in-destination transportation apply as well to getting back to the airport or transport depot to return home. The key here is to remember that once you are on the plane, bus, or ship, it will be difficult to recover anything you have left behind, including your online credentials.

Make sure to take digital inventory of your devices and compare them with the inventory you took prior to leaving on your travel—do the serial numbers match? Are all the programs working correctly and are all data and files accessible? Clear out any volatile memory and cache from your devices and make sure encryption is on. Back up any new data files on a separate flash drive and securely put it away in a safe place that you will remember in your carry-on luggage. Also make sure to secure any hardware locks or keys on your devices. If you used any hotel or third-party computers, make sure you delete the cookie and browsing history to clear any digital traces of you and your data.

As you check out of the hotel or other lodgings secure the receipt for your bill (which contains financial information) and watch your devices as you finalize your bill. If you are using a taxi or shuttle, limit any use of public Wi-Fi or connections available in the vehicle and make sure to check you take everything with you when you get to the depot.

CUSTOMS AND BORDER CONTROLS

When I was crossing the border into Canada, they asked if I had any firearms with me. I said, "Well, what do you need?"

—Stephen Wright[3]

Considering the current state of affairs and the potential for any-thing happening at any time, all countries are concerned with security at their transportation hubs. Keep this in mind as you plan for your arrival at their airport or depot and give yourself enough time so you

---

[2]Goodreads Quotes About Time. <http://www.goodreads.com/quotes/tag/time> [accessed 06/26/2014].
[3]ThinkExist.com. Quotes on borders, <http://thinkexist.com/quotes/with/keyword/border/> [accessed 06/26/2014].

won't miss your flight or train. Some countries require you to pay an exit fee or fill out additional exit paperwork.

You will also be required to submit to security checks that differ from what you experience in the United States. At Tel Aviv's Ben-Gurion airport, for example, passengers go through a series of screenings and interviews in lieu of dumping out their liquids and submitting to full body scanners.[4]

You may be requested again to decrypt your data on your devices and show them to the security officer. Make sure to have proof that you brought your equipment into the country and that you did not purchase it in the country to prevent paying additional tariffs, taxes, or fees. Keep track of your devices to prevent malware being installed or a tracking or spying device. Check your devices when they are returned to you if they were out of your purview for any length of time.

Some airports in an effort to subsidize the increase need of more effective security measures are passing on the cost to the passengers. In Thailand, the Department of Civil Aviation approved a charge to airline passengers of Bt50 for a preboard surveillance check. The fee is to cover the cost of a new Advanced Passenger Processing System to "shorten the immigration process." "Although it may not shorten queues at immigration, it will transfer passenger information at time they check in to international data banks to verify the right to travel and alert security officers if the passenger is on an antiterrorists or criminal blacklist."[5]

ARRIVE BACK IN HOME COUNTRY

People move around so much in the world, things get lost.
—Emma Donoghue[6]

The quote above is very true when it comes to travel—things get lost or misplaced or forgotten. That is why digital inventories are so helpful when we want to ensure we brought back everything we took with us.

---

[4]Berman J. The Huffington Post, U.S. Airport Security is "Just a Show," Experts Say, <http://www.huffingtonpost.com/2013/12/23/airport-security_n_4494308.html>; December 23, 2013.
[5]Ngamsangchaikit W. Security checks on passenger data w/fee, <http://www.ttrweekly.com/site/2013/06/security-checks-on-passenger-data/>; June 24, 2013.
[6]Donoghue E. Room; 2010.

Coming back into the United States is not without its own challenges sometimes. You will need to go through US Customs and Transportation Security Administration (TSA) agents. Nick Lowe, regional director of Northern Europe for Check Point, says one of the riskiest countries to enter with a computing device is the United States. "In summer 2008, the US Department of Homeland Security confirmed that border agents are allowed to search through files on laptops, Blackberries, smartphones, or any other digital device when you enter the country, even when there is no reasonable cause," says Lowe. "Officials can keep data or the entire computer, copy what they want and share this data with other agencies—and can force you to give the password if the data is encrypted. Of course, if the data is not suspicious, guidelines say the copied data should be destroyed—but after what time interval? And how securely will it be stored while it's being assessed?"[7]

You may need to reset your mobile devices for your home-country provider. Make sure Wi-Fi access is off while at the airport or depot so that data on your devices are not accessible to anyone in the public terminal areas that may set up an "evil twin" network to the airport's network that unsuspecting travelers log onto.

BACK TO THE OFFICE

The thrill of coming home has never changed.
—Guy Pearce[8]

The first time you activate, open or start your digital device upon returning from your international travel do not have it connect automatically to any of your networks. Run an antivirus software scan your entire system. Make sure the software is up-to-date before you run it or it may not find the latest malware programs.[9] See Table 5.1[10] for a listing of mobile security and antivirus apps.

---

[7]Computer Weekly. Top five data security travel issues: protect sensitive information on business trips, <http://www.computerweekly.com/feature/Top-five-data-security-travel-issues-Protect-sensitive-information-on-business-trips>; October 2009.
[8]BrainyQuotes, <http://www.brainyquote.com/quotes/keywords/coming_home.html> [accessed 06/26/2014].
[9]Kellly PJ. 5 Tips for cyber security on the road, <http://www.afcea.org/content/?q=node/11834>; October 10, 2013.
[10]For a ranking and detailed review of most of these apps see, <http://mobile-security-software-review.toptenreviews.com> [accessed 06/26/2014].

Table 5.1 Mobile Security and Antivirus Apps

Name	Compatible Devices	URL	Price
Lookout	iOS, Android, Kindle	https://www.lookout.com	Free
FSecure	Android, Tablet	http://www.f-secure.com/en/web/ home_us/mobile-security	$29.99/year
McAfee Mobile Security	iOS, Android, & Amazon	https://www.mcafeemobilesecurity.com	Free
Kapersky Internet Security	iOS & Android	http://bit.ly/1o6Feur	$69.95/year
Webroot Secure Anywhere	iOS & Android	http://www.webroot.com/us/en/	$15/1 device per year
Avast!	iOS	http://www.avast.com/en-us/free-antivirus-mac	Free
Bitdefender	iOS	http://www.bitdefender.com/solutions/ virus-scanner-for-mac.html	Free

When you do get back to your office or home place, run an antivirus scan on your desktop and review your desktop data to make sure it was not tampered with. Check any e-mail accounts and other online accounts for suspicious activity while you were traveling.

If you changed any of the settings for your digital devices, review them and return them to their pretravel configuration. Another good best practice is to "turn off any services that you enabled specifically to facilitate your work while traveling, update and apply any patches that were released while you were away, and scan any data you brought back for malware."[11]

FOLLOW-UP

Like all great travellers, I have seen more than I remember, and remember more than I have seen.

—*Benjamin Disraeli*[12]

In today's digitally connected world, e-mail is not the only way to stay in contact with the people you meet during your travels. Many foreign professionals use US-based social media networks such as LinkedIn and

[11]Cornell University IT Page. Guidelines for international travel with technology, <http://www.it.cornell.edu/security/data/international-travel.cfm>; [accessed 06/30/2014].

[12]Conned D. 613 Funny, Inspirational and incredibly stupid travel quotes, <http://trekity.com/travel-funinspirational-travel-quotes/> [accessed 05/19/2014].

when permitted Facebook and Twitter. You can connect, friend, and/or follow these international associates as you would your colleague in the next cubicle or office. Make sure to connect with only those you feel are appropriate to connect with or that you feel comfortable connecting with a particular social network. For example, you may limit those you "friend" on Facebook because of its more personal nature than those you connect with on LinkedIn, a more professional platform.

Another thing to keep in mind is that foreigners will contact you when you return—even those you did not meet while you were traveling or do not know in any capacity. You will need to determine if these contacts pose any risk to you or your company.[13] For example, consider if the individual was "virtually" introduced by an individual you did meet and/or know from overseas. You can do a quick Google or LinkedIn search on the individual to get a better sense of who they are before you respond to them. If not sure, do not respond at all and delete as it can be a scam or fraud attempt.

THE FUTURE OF TRAVEL SECURITY: ONLINE AND OFF

In late 2013, Expedia released a report regarding the future of travel. The report offers insight into five specific areas:

1. The paradigm shift of "service" to "self-service"
2. Travel to become personal again
3. Transforming big data to smart data
4. Collaboration and content creation
5. New markets, new travelers

The report had a heavy focus on millennials and their use of technology. "For Millennials, service doesn't mean having someone else help you as much as having something help you," says the report. "For this generation, technology, particularly mobile, is their personal assistant, enabling them to stay in touch, ensuring they remember their meetings or friends' birthdays, telling them when to be where and how to get there. Millennials want to cut through the clutter, preferring brands and services which save them time,

---

[13]FBI. Safety and security for the business professional traveling abroad, <http://www.fbi.gov/about-us/investigate/counterintelligence/business-travel-brochure> [accessed 06/26/2014].

and ones that make life and "life on the road" easier and more enjoyable.[14]

Expedia's report goes on to say that because of these changes in passenger behavior with technology in order to secure travel services, travel companies need to take heed and begin to develop new platforms to provide a more collaborative, personalized, and more flexible travel experience.[15]

I end this book with the report's description of a possible future scenario of what we will experience when we travel in the future:

Passengers glide, with their e-passports and smart visas, through terminals uninterrupted by checkpoints and not held up by queues; the journey monitored by sensors that 'talk' to their requisite personal device. At certain touchpoints, like immigration and security, they might encounter automated kiosks for biometric identification that use face, fingerprint, iris or voice ID. A virtual personal assistant stores the traveler's tickets and handles their real-time-updatable itinerary, along with all boarding passes and hotel check-in information. Any delays are automatically relayed to the relevant hotels, car-rental firms or cruise operators.[16]

Let us also envision a future when at each step of the way in this possible scenario, controls are in place to provide security and privacy for this digital trail of breadcrumbs you are leaving behind.

●●●──

Checklist: Return and Follow-Up

- Before departing hotel or lodging do inventory check of all property, especially digital equipment, laptop, mobile, power adapters, cables, etc.
- If you have used any hotel or third-party digital equipment, make sure you are logged out and delete the cookie and browsing histories.
- Clear our any cache memory from your digital devices.
- When you return to your office run an antivirus scan of all your digital devices—including smartphone, tablet, and laptop
- Reset passwords for accounts accessed overseas.

[14]Expedia Inc. The future of travel, <http://expediablog.co.uk/wp-content/uploads/2013/10/Future-of-Travel-Report1.pdf>; 2013.
[15]Gulliver, The Economist Blog. The automated passenger, <http://www.economist.com/blogs/gulliver/2013/10/future-travel>; October 16, 2013.
[16]Expedia. The future of travel, <http://expediablog.co.uk/wp-content/uploads/2013/10/Future-of-Travel-Report1.pdf>; October 2013.

- Check with your company IT department if they have any special procedures for when you return from international travel.
- Check your online accounts for any suspicious activity (especially your financial accounts).
- Only follow-up with individuals you met abroad personally.
- Be cautious of e-mail or other digital communications from foreign individuals from the country or countries you have just returned from. Do not click on any links if you do not know the source especially in text messages.

Printed and bound by CPI Group (UK) Ltd, Croydon, CR0 4YY

03/10/2024

01040426-0005